本書は、1987年刊行『日本人に共通する英語のミス121』、2006年刊行『日本人に共通する英語のミス151〔増補改訂版〕』の新装版です。

はじめに

私は日本で英語を教えていて、たくさんの生徒が長年英語を勉強しているのにもかかわらず、いつも決まった間違いを再三していることに気がつきました。この間違いのうちのあるものは、英語と日本語との文法的相違によるものです。例えば、生徒は、英語で複数形を使うことをよく忘れますが、それは日本語の名詞の単数形と複数形がたいてい同一であるからで、そのためにI love animal.のような間違った文を作ってしまうのです(Common Mistake 1 参照)。また、ある間違いは、1つの日本語の単語に対応する英単語をたった1つしか習わなかったことから起こるものです。例えば「狭い」を英語にするとき、前後関係によりnarrow, small, crampedの3つの単語のどれにもなり得ます。しかし、生徒はたいてい、「狭い」の訳としてnarrowという単語しか覚えていないので、My room is narrow.というような変な文を作ることになってしまうのです(Common Mistake 68 参照)。

さらに日本人に共通する間違いのうちいくつかは、中学校や高校での誤った教え方によるものだったり、間違いや旧式の英語が多い教科書と和英辞典を使っているからだということがわかりました。例えば、「恐ろしい」「怖い」はterribleと学校で学ぶ生徒が多く、ほとんどの辞書では、「恐ろしい」はterribleとしてあるので、本来はI was frightened.と言うべきところを、生徒の作る文がI was terrible.となってしまうのです(Common Mistake 75 参照)。

本書には、私が気づいた日本の大学生や大学を卒業した人の間違いの中から、共通して頻繁に繰り返される151の間違いを集めました。そして特に、不注意による間違いよりも、理解不足によって起こる間違いを選びました。

本書は、旧版の『日本人に共通する英語のミス121』、『日本人に共通する英語のミス151　増補改訂版』の新装版です。読者が自分の英語の間違いに気づき、ミスをなくすために、本書が役立つことを願っています。

2020年9月

著者

Introduction

While I have been teaching in English in Japan, I have noticed that many of my students make certain basic mistakes again and again, even though they have been studying English for many years. Some of these mistakes are caused by the grammatical differences between English and Japanese. For example, students often forget to use the plural in English because in Japanese nouns are usually the same in both singular and plural, and so they produce incorrect sentences such as 'I love animal'. (See Common Mistake 1). Other mistakes occur because students have learned only one equivalent for a Japanese word. For example, the Japanese word *semai* can be translated as either 'narrow', or 'small' or 'cramped', depending on the context, but high school students usually learn only word 'narrow' as a translation for *semai*, and so they produce strange sentences such as 'My room is narrow', (See Common Mistake 68).

In addition, I have realized that some of the common mistakes of Japanese students are caused by wrong teaching in high schools, and by the use of textbooks and Japanese-English dictionaries which are full of wrong and old-fashioned English. For example, many students learn at school that the English for *osoroshii* and *kowai* is 'terrible', and most dictionaries say *osoroshii* equals 'terrible', so students produce sentences such as 'I was terrible' when they should say 'I was frightened'. (See Common Mistake 75)

In this book I have collected 151 of the most common mistakes which I have noticed being made by Japanese students and university graduates. In particular, I have chosen those mistakes which are caused by a lack of understanding, rather than by carelessness. This book is a new edition of my former books, '121 Common Mistakes of Japanese Students of English' and '151 Common Mistakes of Japanese Students of English'. I hope the book will help students of English to recognize their mistakes, and then eliminate them.

謝辞

本書の元となった書籍の執筆にご協力いただき、たくさんの助言をしていただいた松井美枝子先生、オバーン・テイラー先生、ラルフ・ボズマン先生、デイビッド・メアー先生に感謝の意を捧げます。長年にわたる日本での英語教育経験に基づいた諸先生方の助言のおかげで、書籍がよりよいものになりました。そして、私にそもそものヒントを与えてくれた私の生徒全員にも感謝の意を表します。彼らの間違いや質問が本書を作り上げたのです。また、根気よく注意深く編集をしてくださった、伊藤秀樹さんをはじめとするジャパンタイムズ出版の方々に感謝いたします。さらに、最初に執筆を勧めてくれた義父の武林英二と、常に私の力となってくれた妻の康子にも謝辞を贈ります。

Acknowledgments

I would like to thank Mieko Matsui, O'Byrne Taylor, Ralph Bosman and David Mair for their help in creating earlier versions of this book and making many valuable comments and suggestions. Their comments, based on many years' experience of teaching English in Japan have greatly improved the book. I also wish to thank all my Japanese students, as it is their mistakes and questions which have given rise to this book. In addition, I would like to thank Hideki Ito and all the editorial staff of the Japan Times Publishing for their patient and careful editing. Finally, I must thank my father-in-law, Eiji Takebayashi, for originally suggesting that I write a book, and also for my wife, Yasko, for encouraging and helping me at every stage of writing it.

James H. M. Webb

Chapter 3 | 動詞に関する間違い
Problems with Verbs

Common Mistake

Chapter 4 | 形容詞・副詞に関する間違い
Problems with Adjectives and Adverbs

Common Mistake

Chapter 5 | 名詞に関する間違い
Problems with Nouns

Common Mistake

Chapter 6 | 前置詞・接続詞に関する間違い
Problems with Prepositions and Conjunctions

Common Mistake

Chapter 7 | その他の間違い
Miscellaneous Problems

Common Mistake

カバーデザイン　小口翔平＋三沢稜（tobufune）
本文デザイン・DTP　（有）ディーイーピー
DTP　（株）創樹
編集協力　堀内友子（増補改訂版時）

Chapter 1

複数形に関する間違い

Problems with Plurals

Common Mistake 1

✕1 I hate cockroach.

✕2 English newspaper is difficult to read.

✕3 Japanese people like thing which comes from foreign country.

ある特定のものを指すのではなく、一般的な意味でものについて話すときは、ふつう数えられる名詞の複数形を使います。

When we talk about things in general, we usually use the plural with countable nouns.

① **I hate cockroaches.**

私は〈特定のゴキブリではなく一般的に〉ゴキブリが嫌いです。

② **English newspapers are difficult to read.**

〈The Japan Times, the Guardianなど特定の新聞を指すのではなく、どれでも〉英字新聞は難しい。

③ **Japanese people like things which come from foreign countries.**

日本人は〈どこの国の何と特定しないで〉外国から入ってくるものが好きです。

一般的な意味でものについて話すもう1つの方法は、数えられる名詞の単数形の前にaかtheをつけることです。《the＋単数形》は学術書や講義の中で、また科学や科学技術に関して話すときによく使われます。

Another way of talking about things in general is to use 'a' or 'the' before a singular countable noun. 'The' + a singular noun is commonly used in academic books and lectures, and when talking about science and technology.

● **A** motorbike is cheaper than a car.
オートバイは車より安い。

● **The** television was invented by a Scotsman.
テレビはスコットランド人が発明したものです。

しかし、数えられる名詞を一般的な意味で使う際のもっともふつうの方法は、冠詞なしの複数形を用いることです。
However, the commonest way of making general statements about countable nouns is to use the plural with no article.

Common Mistake 2

✕1 American people is bigger than Japanese people.

✕2 The police was very slow and inefficient.

✕3 This pants is very comfortable.

✕4 I bought a trousers.

✕5 Where is the scissors?

✕6 Glasses is expensive.

people はふつう、複数形で用いられ、police, pants, trousers (pants はアメリカ英語、trousers はイギリス英語), jeans, pajamas, scissors, glasses (メガネ) などは常に複数形として扱わなければならない名詞です。**これらの名詞が主語のとき、動詞は is/was/has ではなく are/were/have でなければなりません。また、これらの名詞の前には、単数を表す a, this, that は用いられません。**

'People' is usually plural, and 'police', 'pants', 'trousers', 'jeans', 'pajamas', 'scissors', 'glasses' are always plural. Therefore, if one of these words is the subject of a sentence, we must say 'are' instead of 'is', 'were' instead of 'was' and 'have' instead of 'has'. Also, we cannot put 'a', 'this' or 'that' in front of them.

① **American people are bigger than Japanese people.**
アメリカ人は日本人より大きい。

② **The police were very slow and inefficient.**
警察はやることが遅くて非能率的でした。

③ **These pants are very comfortable.**
このズボンは、とてもはき心地がよい。

④ **I bought some trousers.** (イギリス英語)
私はズボンを買いました。

⑤ **Where are the scissors?**
ハサミはどこにありますか。

⑥ **Glasses are expensive.**
メガネは高い。

Common Mistake 3

~~1~~ We ate a lot of delicious foods.

~~2~~ My mother gave me some fruits.

~~3~~ I have a lot of homeworks.

~~4~~ My father often gives me good advices.

~~5~~ I need to buy some furnitures.

foodとfruitはふつう、数えられない単数の名詞です。homework, housework, advice, information, knowledge, furnitureは常に数えられない単数の名詞です。

'Food' and 'fruit' are usually uncountable and singular. 'Homework', 'housework', 'advice', 'information', 'knowledge' and 'furniture' are always uncountable and singular.

1. **We ate a lot of delicious food.**
   私たちはたくさんおいしい食べ物を食べました。
2. **My mother gave me some fruit.**
   母が私に果物をくれました。
3. **I have a lot of homework.**
   宿題がいっぱいあります。
4. **My father often gives me good advice.**
   父はよくいい助言をしてくれます。
5. **I need to buy some furniture.**
   家具を買わなければなりません。

foods, fruitsという言い方もありますが、日常の英語ではあまり使われません。

The words 'foods' and 'fruits' exist, but they are not common in everyday English.

Common Mistake 4

1. ~~Japanese people eat a lot of fishes.~~
2. ~~I eat chickens almost every day.~~
3. ~~Americans eat a lot of meats.~~

食べ物のfishとchickenは、常に単数で数えられない名詞です。meatは、ふつうは単数で数えられない名詞です。

The words 'fish' and 'chicken' are always singular and uncountable when they refer to food, and the word 'meat' is usually singular and uncountable.

1. **Japanese people eat a lot of fish.**
日本人は魚をたくさん食べます。

2. **I eat chicken almost every day.**
私はほとんど毎日とり肉を食べます。

3. **Americans eat a lot of meat.**
アメリカ人は肉をたくさん食べます。

食べ物ではなく、水に住む生物としてのfishは数えられる名詞ですが、複数形はfishesではなく、fishがふつうです。fishesという語も存在しますが、現代の英語ではほとんど使われません。

'Fish' is a countable noun when it means the creature which lives in water, rather than a kind of food. The plural is usually 'fish', not 'fishes'. The word 'fishes' exists, but it is not common in modern English.

● I caught three fish.
私は魚を3匹釣りました。

● We went diving and saw hundreds of beautiful fish.
私たちはダイビングに行って、とてもたくさんの美しい魚を見ました。

chickenの基本的な意味は「メスのにわとり」です。これは数えられる名詞で、複数形はchickensです。
The basic meaning of 'chicken' is 'hen'. This is a countable noun, and the plural is 'chickens'.

● My parents keep chickens.
両親はにわとりを飼っています。

Common Mistake 5

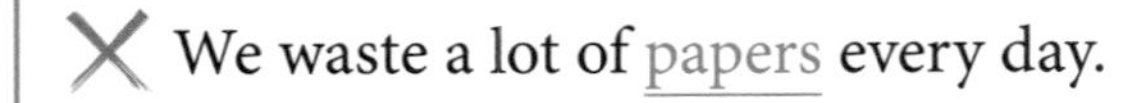

paperは、ものを書いたり、印刷したり、包んだりするための素材としての「紙」という意味で使われるときは、数えられない名詞です。
'Paper' is an uncountable noun when it has its basic meaning of a material used for writing, printing, wrapping, etc.

We waste a lot of paper every day.
私たちは毎日たくさんの紙を無駄にしています。

paperが数えられる名詞になるのは、次のような意味を持つ場合です。a) 新聞、b) 書類、証明書（ふつうは複数形）、c) 評論または学問的な論文。
'Paper' is a countable noun when it has one of the following meanings: (a) a newspaper, (b) (usually plural) documents, (c) an essay or scholarly dissertation.

● Diana's face was in the papers almost every day.
ダイアナの顔（写真）は、ほとんど毎日のように新聞に載っていました。

● The police asked to see my papers.
警察官は私に証明書を見せるよう言いました。

- He has written several **papers** about ancient Greek hairpins.
  彼は古代ギリシャのヘアピンについての**論文**をいくつか書きました。

Common Mistake 6

 Japan imports many woods.

木材はwoodと言い、数えられない名詞です。

The material which we get from trees is called ‘wood’, and this is an uncountable noun.

 **Japan imports a lot of wood.**

日本はたくさんの木材を輸入しています。

森はイギリス英語ではwood、アメリカ英語ではwoodsと言います。**woodはforestよりも小さい森のことです。**この意味で使われるときのwoodは数えられる名詞です。

A place where many trees are growing is called a ‘wood’ in British English, or ‘woods’ in American English. A wood is smaller than a forest. ‘Wood’ is a countable noun when it has this meaning.

- I love walking in the **woods**.
  私は**森**を歩くのが大好きです。〈アメリカ英語〉

- There’s a **wood** behind my house.
  私の家の裏は**森**です。〈イギリス英語〉

Common Mistake 7

✗1 She is one of the most popular actress in Japan.

✗2 He is one of my best friend.

one of ～(～のうちの1つ) のあとには、必ず複数形の名詞がきます。
'One of' is always followed by a plural noun.

1. **She is one of the most popular actresses in Japan.**
   彼女は、日本でもっとも人気のある女優の1人です。
2. **He is one of my best friends.**
   彼は私のもっとも親しい友人の1人です。

Exercise 1

次の文中の間違いを見つけて正しい英語に直してください。文末のかっこ内の数は、間違いの数を示しています。答えは巻末にあります。

1. Japanese train is often crowded. (2)

2. I love peach. (1)

3. Japanese people is always busy. (1)

4. She always wears a jeans. (1)

5. I was very busy doing homeworks in the vacation. (1)

6. Fruits is very expensive. (1)

7. The police has not caught the murderer yet. (1)

8. It is one of the most beautiful place I have ever visited. (1)

9. I like all kinds of food—meats, fishes, vegetables, etc. (2)

10. I eat fried chickens almost every day. (1)

11. The number of fishes in the world's oceans is decreasing. (1)

____

12. I always try not to waste papers. (1)

____

13. House, furnitures, newspapers, magazines and books are all made from woods. (3)

____

Chapter 2

冠詞に関する間違い

Problems with Articles

Common Mistake 8

~~1~~ I want to buy ∧ car.

~~2~~ We went to ∧ bar and had ∧ drink.

~~3~~ When I was ∧ child, I had ∧ dog.

~~4~~ Please put it in ∧ refrigerator.

~~5~~ There's someone at ∧ front door.

~~6~~ I live near ∧ sea.

数えられる名詞の単数形の前には、ほとんど常にaかtheをつけます。数えられる名詞の単数形が初めて出てきて、それが指している特定のものや人を聞き手が知らないときは、aをつけます。

We nearly always put 'a' or 'the' before singular countable nouns. We put 'a' before a singular countable noun when it is mentioned for the first time, and the listener does not know the particular thing or person we are referring to.

1. **I want to buy a car.**
   私は車を買いたい。
2. **We went to a bar and had a drink.**
   私たちはバーへ行って1杯飲みました。
3. **When I was a child, I had a dog.**
   子どものころ犬を飼っていました。

何のことを指しているのか聞き手が知っているときや、明らかな場合は、名詞の前にtheをつけます。**たいていの家は、玄関は1つ、冷蔵庫も1つだけあるのがふつうなので、次の例文では、どの玄関、どの冷蔵庫のことを指しているのか明らかです。したがってtheが使われます。また太陽は1つしかなく、どの太陽か考えなくても明らかなので、the sunと言います。これと同じ理由でthe sea, the moon, the world, the Emperorと言います。**

We use 'the' before a noun if the listener knows what we are referring to, or if it is obvious what we are referring to. Most houses have only one refrigerator and one front door, so in the sentences below it is obvious which refrigerator and which front door the speaker is referring to. Therefore, 'the' is used. Also, we usually think that there is only one sun, so we say 'the sun'. For the same reason, we say 'the sea', 'the moon', 'the world', 'the Emperor', etc.

4 **Please put it in the refrigerator.**
それを冷蔵庫に入れてください。

5 **There's someone at the front door.**
玄関のところにだれかがいます。

6 **I live near the sea.**
私は海の近くに住んでいます。

数えられる名詞が2度目に出てきたときは、どれを指すのかがわかっているので、名詞の前にtheをつけます。

We also use 'the' before a noun when it is mentioned for the second time, because then the listener knows what the speaker is referring to.

- I bought a shirt and a jacket. The shirt is blue and the jacket is brown.
  私はシャツと上着を買いました。シャツはブルーで、上着は茶色です。

Common Mistake 9

✕1 I like listening to the music.

✕2 I love the nature.

✕3 I like the cats better than the dogs.

数えられない名詞、数えられる名詞の複数形が、一般的な意味で使われているときは、名詞の前にtheはつけません。
We do not use 'the' before an uncountable noun or a plural noun when it has a general meaning.

1 **I like listening to ∧ music.**
私は音楽〈特定な音楽ではなく音楽全般〉を聞くのが好きです。

2 **I love ∧ nature.**
私は自然が好きです。

3 **I like ∧ cats better than ∧ dogs.**
私は犬より猫が好きです。

数えられない名詞、数えられる名詞の複数形が一般的な意味ではなく、特定のものを指す場合はtheを使います。
We use 'the' before uncountable nouns and plural nouns when they do not have a general meaning.

- What's the music you were playing just now?
  さっきかけていた音楽は何ですか。
- The dogs in this neighborhood are very noisy.
  この近所の犬はとてもうるさい。

Common Mistake 10

~~1~~ We had a terrible weather.

~~2~~ We saw a beautiful scenery.

~~3~~ I got a good news.

数えられない名詞の前にaをつけることはありません。例えば、weather, scenery, news, information, furniture, travel, luggage, baggage（luggageはイギリス英語、baggageはアメリカ英語）、advice, health, research, progressなどは数えられない名詞です。ただし、a piece of news / information / adviceという言い方はできます。

We never use 'a' before uncountable nouns, for example 'weather', 'scenery', 'news', 'information', 'furniture', 'travel', 'luggage', 'baggage', 'advice', 'health', 'research' and 'progress'. However, we can say 'a piece of news/information/advice'.

1 **We had ∧ terrible weather.**

ひどい天候でした。

2 **We saw some beautiful scenery.**

私たちは美しい景色を見ました。

3 **I got some good news.**

いいニュースがあります。

I got a good piece of news.

1ついい知らせを受け取りました。

Common Mistake 11

~~1~~ We had a lunch in a French restaurant.

~~2~~ We had a dinner together.

breakfast, lunch, dinnerなどの食事を表す語の前には、aやtheをつけません。

We do not use 'a' or 'the' before the names of meals.

① **We had ∧ lunch in a French restaurant.**

私たちはフランス料理店で昼食をとりました。

② **We had ∧ dinner together.**

私たちは一緒に夕食を食べました。

この決まりには2つの例外があります。1つは、食事を表す語の前に形容詞があるときで、aをつけます。

There are two exceptions to this rule. Firstly, we can use 'a' before the name of a meal if it is preceded by an adjective.

- We had **a** wonderful dinner in a French restaurant.
  私たちはフランス料理店ですばらしい食事をしました。
- We had **a** light supper at 6 o'clock.
  私たちは6時に軽い夕食を食べました。

もう1つの例外は、食事を表す語のあとにそれを修飾する節があるときで、theをつけます。

Secondly, we can use 'the' before the name of a meal if it is followed by a clause which qualifies it.

- **The** lunch he cooked for us was very strange.
  彼が私たちに作ってくれた昼食は、とても珍しいものでした。

● I didn't like the breakfast we were served.
私たちに出された朝食が、私は好きではありませんでした。

Common Mistake 12

~~1~~ I have lived in ∧ same house all my life.

~~2~~ Women should get ∧ same pay as men if they do ∧ same work.

sameの前には常にtheが必要です。
We always say 'the' before 'same'.

1. **I have lived in the same house all my life.**
私は生まれてからずっと同じ家に住んでいます。

2. **Women should get the same pay as men if they do the same work.**
女性が男性と同じ仕事をするのなら、同じ報酬を得るべきです。

Common Mistake 13

✗1 Japan was defeated in ∧ Second World War.

✗2 Japan was defeated in the World War II.

「第二次世界大戦」と言うとき、Second World Warの前にはtheをつけますが、World War IIの前にはtheをつけません。

We use 'the' before 'Second World War', but not before 'World War II'.

1 **Japan was defeated in the Second World War.**

2 **Japan was defeated in ∧ World War II.**

日本は第二次世界大戦で敗れました。

Exercise 2

次の文中の間違いを見つけて正しい英語に直してください。文末のかっこ内の数は、間違いの数を示しています。答えは巻末にあります。

1. When I was high school student, I belonged to baseball club. (2)

 ____

2. Last summer I had part-time job as waitress in restaurant. (3)

 ____

3. We stayed in small hotel by sea. (2)

 ____

4. Please put it on top shelf of cupboard. (2)

 ____

5. We had a dinner in Italian restaurant. (2)

 ____

6. I'll wait for you at entrance of cinema. (2)

 ____

7. My father gave me a good advice. (1)

 ____

8. I am same height as my mother. (1)

 ____

9. My parents were born before the World War II. (1)

 ____

Chapter 3

動詞に関する間違い

Problems with Verbs

Common Mistake 14

✕1 When I saw this film, I knew the importance of love.

✕2 I knew many interesting things by reading this book.

knowは「知識がある」「知っている」という意味です。「知識を得る」「知る」と言いたい場合はlearn, realize, discoverを使います。

'Know' means 'have knowledge'. 'Learn', 'realize' and 'discover' mean 'gain knowledge'.

1. **When I saw this film, I realized the importance of love.**
   この映画を見たとき、愛の大切さを知りました。
2. **I learned many interesting things by reading this book.**
   この本を読んで多くの興味深いことを学びました。

Common Mistake 15

✗1 Please teach me your phone number.

✗2 Could you teach me the way to the station, please?

電話番号、住所、道順などの単なる情報を伝えるときは、teachではなくtellを使って次のように言います。

We do not use 'teach' for pieces of information such as telephone numbers, addresses, directions, etc., so we should say:

1. **Please tell me your phone number.**
   あなたの電話番号を教えてください。
2. **Could you tell me the way to the station, please?**
   駅までの道を教えてください。

teachには2つの主な使い方があります。1つは学問や知識を「教える」と言う場合です。

'Teach' has two main uses. Firstly, we can say that someone teaches an academic subject or a field of knowledge, or an aspect or an academic subject or field of knowledge.

- I teach history.
  私は歴史を教えています。
- Mr. Jackson taught me the difference between 'look' and 'watch'.
  ジャクソン先生は私にlookとwatchの違いを教えてくれました。

もう1つは技術や方法を「教える」と言う場合です。

Secondly, we can say that someone teaches a technique, or how to do something.

● My mother taught me how to cook.

母が料理を教えてくれました。

Common Mistake 16

✗1 My girlfriend always wins me at tennis.

✗2 Our team played well, but the other team won us.

💡「試合や戦いに勝つ」はwin a gameまたはwin a fightですが、試合や戦いの相手である「人やチームに勝つ」はbeat a personまたはbeat a teamです。

One 'wins' a game or fight, but one 'beats' the person or team one is playing or fighting against.

① My girlfriend always beats me at tennis.

僕のガールフレンドはいつもテニスで僕に勝ちます。

② Our team played well, but the other team beat us.

私たちのチームはよくやりましたが、相手のチームに敗れました。

Common Mistake 17

 My parents didn't admit me to go to America.

admitは「許可を与える」という意味ではありません。「許可を与える」はletやallowです。

'Admit' does not mean 'give permission'. 'Let' and 'allow' mean 'give permission'.

My parents didn't let me go to America.
My parents didn't allow me to go to America.
両親は私をアメリカへ行かせてくれませんでした。

動詞admitには2つの主な意味があります。

'Admit' has two main meanings:

1. 何かが真実であると認めること（ふつうは何かよくないこと）。
   To state or agree that something is true (usually something bad):
   - I admit I was wrong.
     私は自分が悪かったと認めます。
   - He admitted stealing the money.
     彼はお金を盗んだことを認めました。
2. 人が中に入ることを許すこと。
   To allow someone to enter:
   - The government should admit more immigrants.
     政府はもっと外国からの移民を認めるべきです。

Common Mistake 18

~~1~~ I think this job fits me.

~~2~~ Pink doesn't fit me.

職業や色、場所などが人に「合う」と言うときは、fitではなくsuitを使います。
We say that a job, color, place, etc., 'suits' a person.

1. **I think this job suits me.**
   この仕事は私に合っていると思います。
2. **Pink doesn't suit me.**
   ピンクは私には似合いません。

fitは服や靴などの「サイズや形が合う」という意味です。
The verb 'fit' means 'be the right size and shape'.

- These shoes fit perfectly.
  この靴はピッタリです。
- This coat fits me perfectly, but I don't think it suits me.
  このコートはサイズはちょうどいいけれど、私には似合わないと思います。

Common Mistake 19

✕1 I wish you pass the exam.

✕2 I wish you will be very happy together.

未来のことについて「～であるといいと思います」と節を使って言いたいときの動詞は、wishではなくてhopeです。**I hopeのあとの名詞節は、内容が未来であっても現在形をよく使います。**

We do not use 'wish' followed by a clause to talk about the future. Instead, we say 'hope'. After 'I hope' we often use a verb in the present tense, even though the meaning is future.

① **I hope you pass the exam.**

試験に受かるといいですね。

② **I hope you will be very happy together.**

お二人がとても幸せでありますように。

現在や過去のことが、実際と違っていることを願って「～だといいなあと思います」と言うときは、wishと名詞節を使って表現します。**その場合、名詞節の動詞の時制は、現在のことは過去に、過去のことは過去完了になります（仮定法）。**

We use 'wish' followed by a clause to say that we would like a present situation or a past situation to be different.

- I wish I had longer legs.
  私の脚がもっと長ければいいのに。【実際は短い】
- I wish it wasn't raining.
  雨が降っていなければいいのになあ。【実際は降っている】
- I wish I had never met you.
  あなたに出会わなければよかったのに。【実際は出会った】

相手の幸運を願うときも、2つの目的語と一緒にwishを使います。

We also use 'wish' followed by two objects to say that we hope someone has good luck or happiness in the future.

- I **wish** you good luck.
  幸運を祈ります。
- I **wish** you a merry Christmas.
  メリークリスマス／あなたにとって楽しいクリスマスでありますように。

Common Mistake 20

✗1 I'm very bad at writing pictures.

✗2 He wrote a map to show where his house was.

ペンや鉛筆で絵や地図を描くのはdrawです。writeは文字を書くときのみに使います。

'Draw' means 'make a picture or map with a pen or pencil'. 'Write' is only used for words.

① **I'm very bad at drawing pictures.**
私は絵を描くのがとても苦手です。

② **He drew a map to show where his house was.**
彼は自分の家の場所を示す地図を描きました。

Common Mistake 21

✕1 I became to like him.

✕2 I gradually became to be able to speak English.

✕3 We came not to see each other so often.

「〜するようになる」と言う場合、動詞の前にはbecomeではなくbeginを使います。次に形容詞がくるならbecomeです。

'Become' cannot be used before a verb. In sentences such as these we use 'begin' before a verb, or 'become' before an adjective.

① **I began to like him.**

私は彼を好きになりました。

② **I gradually became able to speak English.**

私はだんだん英語が話せるようになりました。

いくつかの動詞、例えばrealize, like, love, hateなどの前には、beginの代わりにcomeを使うことができます。しかしほとんどの動詞の前ではbeginもしくはbeginの反対の意味であるstopを使います。

'Come' can mean 'begin' before a small number of verbs, such as 'realize', 'like', 'love', 'hate', etc. Before most verbs, however, it is better to say 'begin', or its opposite 'stop'.

③ **We stopped seeing each other so often.**

私たちはあまり頻繁に会わないようになりました。

Common Mistake 22

✕1 He was dead of cancer last year.

✕2 All my grandparents dead.

動詞die（死ぬ）の過去形はdied（死んだ）です。deadは「もう生きていない」という意味の形容詞で、動作ではなく変わらない状態を表しています。

The past tense of 'die' is 'died'. 'Dead' means 'no longer living'. It is an adjective, not a verb, and it describes a non-changing situation, not an action.

1 **He died of cancer last year.**
彼は昨年ガンで死にました。

2 **All my grandparents have died.**
私の祖父母は皆亡くなりました。

All my grandparents are dead.
私の祖父母は皆もういません。

- I've never seen a dead body.
  私は死体を見たことがありません。

He has died. とHe is dead. は同じような意味ですが、前者は最近亡くなったとき、後者は亡くなったのは最近ではないときによく使われます。

'He has died' means the same as 'He is dead' but 'He has died' is more common if the person has died recently, while 'He is dead' is more common if the person has not died recently.

Common Mistake 23

✗1 I borrowed a video from the video store.

✗2 It costs ¥500 to borrow a bicycle for two hours.

アメリカ英語でrentは、お金を払って物を借りることです。イギリス英語でrentは、家やアパートなどを長期間借りることで、hireは自転車や服などを短時間借りることです。

In American English, 'rent' means 'pay money to use something'. In British English, 'rent' is used for things which are used for a long time, such as houses and flats, while 'hire' is used with things which are only used for a short time, e.g. bicycles, clothes, etc.

1 **I rented a video from the video store.**
ビデオ店でビデオを借りました。〈アメリカ英語〉

2 **It costs ¥500 to hire a bicycle for two hours.**
自転車を２時間借りるのに500円かかります。〈イギリス英語〉

borrowは、お金を払わないで物を借りる場合に使います。
We use 'borrow' if we do not pay any money.

● Can I **borrow** your pen?
ペンを貸していただけますか。

Common Mistake 24

✗1 My car slipped on some ice.

✗2 His motorbike slipped on a patch of oil.

車やオートバイ、その他車輪のついた乗り物がスリップしたときは、slip ではなく skid を使います。

The verb 'slip' is not used for cars, motorbikes and other wheeled vehicles. Instead we should say 'skid'.

1. **My car skidded on some ice.**
   私の車は氷の上でスリップしました。
2. **His motorbike skidded on a patch of oil.**
   彼のバイクは油のあるところでスリップしました。

slip は人間や車輪のついていないものがすべったときに使います。

We use 'slip' for people or anything without wheels.

- I slipped on some ice and fell over.
  私は氷の上ですべって転びました。

× My boyfriend presented me some flowers.

友人や親戚の間で「プレゼントをする」と言うときは、give を使います。
We use 'give' to talk about the giving of presents between friends and relatives.

My boyfriend gave me some flowers.
ボーイフレンドが花をくれました。

動詞の present を使うのは、形式的、儀式的な場で賞やメダル、花束などを贈る場合です。
We use the verb 'present' to talk about the giving of prizes, medals, bouquets, etc., at formal, ceremonial occasions.

- The Queen presented the prizes.
  女王は賞を授与しました。
- He was presented with a gold watch when he retired.
  退職に際して、彼は金時計を贈呈されました。

Common Mistake 26

~~1~~ I am often said that I look like my mother.

~~2~~ My sister is often said she is beautiful.

「私は人に～と言われる」はI am told (that) ～です。同じように、「彼女は人に～と言われる」はShe is told (that)～です。

'I am told' means 'people say to me'; 'She is told' means 'people say to her', and so on.

① **I am often told that I look like my mother.**
私は母に似ているとよく言われます。

② **My sister is often told she is beautiful.**
姉はきれいだとよく言われます。

It is said (that) ～ は「～と言われています」という意味です。この形はやや形式的で主に書き言葉として使われます。

'It is said (that)' means 'some people say'. This structure is rather formal, and is used mainly in writing.

- **It is said that** he is living in South America.
彼は南米に住んでいると言われています。

また《He is said＋to不定詞》の形で言うこともできます。これも形式的で主に書き言葉として使われます。

We can also say 'He is said' followed by a to-infinitive. This structure is also rather formal, and is used mainly in writing.

- **He is said to** be living in South America.
彼は南米に住んでいると言われています。

Common Mistake 27

✗1 *A*: What are you going to do after this lesson?
B: I'm going to come home.

✗2 I live in Tokyo now, but I often come back to my hometown in Shizuoka Prefecture.

「帰る」と英語で言うとき、常にcome homeやcome backになるとは限りません。話し手（あるいは聞き手）のいる場所への動きに対してはcomeが使われ、いない場所への動きに対してはgoが使われます。つまり、話し手（あるいは聞き手）が家にいないときはgo homeと言います。

'*Kaeru*' should not always be translated as 'come home' or 'come back'. 'Come' is used for a movement to the place where the speaker or listener is, while 'go' is used for a movement to a place where the speaker and listener are not. In other words, one should say 'go home' if one is not at home now, and if the listener is not at one's home.

① ***A*: What are you going to do after this lesson?**
この授業が終わったらどうするつもりですか。

***B*: I'm going to go home.**
I'm going home.
家に帰ります。

② **I live in Tokyo now, but I often go back to my hometown in Shizuoka Prefecture.**
私は今、東京に住んでいますが、よく静岡県の故郷へ帰ります。

Common Mistake 28

✗1 I like watching paintings in art galleries.

✗2 We went to the park to watch the cherry blossoms.

✗3 He watched his watch.

watchは動いたり変化したりするものや、動いたり変化するかもしれないものを「見る」と言うときに使います。例えば、テレビ、スポーツ、パレード、野鳥や動物などを見るときです。動いたり変化したりしないものを見るときは、look atやseeを使います。look atには、seeよりも注意深く見るという意味合いがあります。

We use 'watch' with things which are moving and changing, or which might begin to move and change. For example, we watch television, sport, parades, wild birds and animals, etc. If something is not moving or changing, we use 'look at' or 'see'. 'Look at' implies more careful attention than 'see'.

1 **I like looking at paintings in art galleries.**

私は美術館で絵を見るのが好きです。

2 **We went to the park to look at the cherry blossoms.**

We went to the park to see the cherry blossoms.

私たちは公園に桜を見に行きました。

watchには、何かをある程度長い間見るという意味合いが含まれています。look atは、何かを（例えば、それが動いたり変化したりしていても）短時間だけ見るときに使います。

The word 'watch' implies that one watches something for some length of time. 'Look at' is used if one looks at something for only a short time (even if it is moving and changing).

He looked at his watch.

彼は時計を見ました。

映画や芝居の公演を「見る」と言うときは、watchではなく、ふつうseeを使います。

We usually use 'see' not 'watch' to talk about public performances of films and plays.

- Shall we go and see a film this weekend?
  週末に映画を見に行きましょうか。

Common Mistake 29

✕ University students have a lot of time to play.

目的語のないplayは、子どもが遊ぶときに使う動詞です。**大人の場合はenjoy oneself, have fun, relaxなどを使います。**

The verb 'play' without an object is used for children, not for university students and adults. Instead we say 'enjoy oneself', 'have fun', 'relax', etc.

〇 **University students have a lot of time to enjoy themselves.**

大学生には遊ぶ時間がたくさんあります。

University students have a lot of free time.

大学生は暇がたくさんあります。

「友達と遊ぶ」(大人の場合)は、meet a friendまたはmeet some friendsと言うことができます。**形式的でない英語では、hang out with a friendとも言えます。**

The Japanese expression *tomodachi to asobu* can be translated as 'meet a friend' or 'meet some friends'. In informal English, one can also say "hang out with a friend".

● I met some friends of mine on Sunday.

日曜日に友達に会いました → 日曜日に友達と遊びました。

しかし大人でも、楽器を「演奏する」とかゲームを「する」と言う場合には、playを使います。

However, we can say that adults 'play' a musical instrument, or 'play' a game.

Common Mistake 30

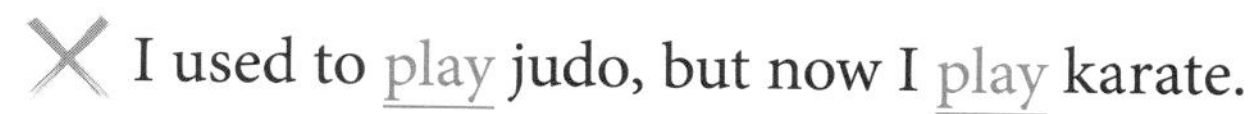

✕ I used to play judo, but now I play karate.

💡 柔道、空手、剣道、相撲、ボクシングなどの格闘技にはplayではなく、doかlearnを使います。

We do not use 'play' with types of fighting, for example, judo, karate, kendo, sumo, boxing, etc. Instead we say 'do' or 'learn'.

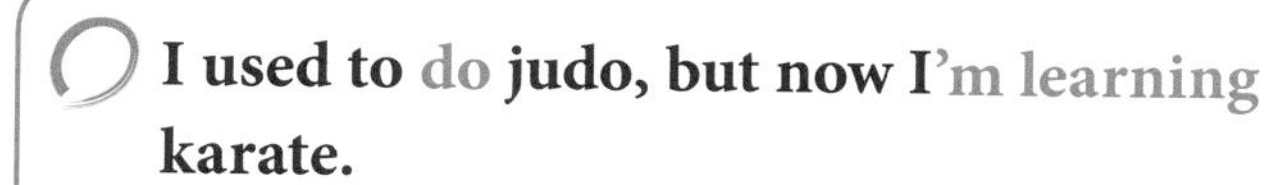

〇 **I used to do judo, but now I'm learning karate.**

昔は柔道をやっていましたが、今は空手を習っています。

Common Mistake 31

~~1~~ When he saw the policeman, he escaped very fast.

~~2~~ A big car hit my car and then escaped very fast.

動詞escapeには３つの主な使い方があります。

The verb 'escape' has three main uses:

1. 閉じ込められた場所（刑務所、火事で燃えている建物、動物園など）から「逃げる」場合。
   One can 'escape' from something confining, such as a prison, a burning house, a zoo, etc.
   - Three prisoners have escaped.
     囚人が３人脱走しました。
   - A tiger has escaped from the zoo.
     トラが動物園から逃げました。

2. 危険なものやとても不愉快なもの（死、災難、追跡者、刑罰など）から「逃れる」場合。このときのescapeの意味は「逃げる」のではなく「避ける」です。
   One can 'escape' from something dangerous or very unpleasant, such as death, a disaster, pursuers, punishment, etc. This meaning of 'escape' is 'avoid' not 'run away'.
   - She narrowly escaped being drowned.
     彼女は、かろうじておぼれずにすみました。
   - The police searched for him, but he managed to escape from them, and left the country.
     警察は彼を追いましたが、彼は何とか逃れて外国へ出ました。

3. ガス、液体などが「漏れる」場合。
   A gas or liquid can 'escape' from its container. The meaning is 'leak out'.
   - Some gas escaped from the pipe.
     パイプからガスが漏れました。

閉じ込められていないところから逃げるときは、escapeではなくrun awayまたは〈動詞＋away〉を使います。

However, if someone is fleeing from something which is not confining, we say 'run away' or use a suitable verb of motion with 'away'. We do not say 'escape'.

① **When he saw the policeman, he ran away very fast.**

警官を見て彼は大急ぎで逃げました。

② **A big car hit my car and then drove away very fast.**

大きな車が私の車にぶつかって、大急ぎで走り去りました。

Common Mistake 32

✗ 1 Most rice and vegetables include agricultural chemicals.

✗ 2 Soft drinks include a lot of sugar.

物体がほかの物体の中にあると言いたいときは、containという動詞を使います。X contains Yの意味は、YがXの中にあるということです。

If we want to say that a physical object is inside another object, we use the verb 'contain'. 'X contains Y' means that Y is inside X.

1 **Most rice and vegetables contain agricultural chemicals.**

ほとんどの米と野菜には農薬が入っています。

2 **Soft drinks contain a lot of sugar.**

ソフトドリンクにはたくさんの砂糖が入っています。

X includes Yの意味は、YはXの一部分、あるいは構成要素であるということです。物理的にYがXの中に入っているという意味ではありません。

'X includes Y' means that Y is one of the parts or components of X. It does not mean that Y is physically inside X.

- The price **includes** tax.
  その値段には税金が含まれています。
- There were 15 people at the party, **including** me.
  パーティには、私を含めて15人が来ていました。

Common Mistake 33

✕1 Japanese men put on black suits and white ties at weddings.

✕2 Before the war most Japanese women put on kimonos.

put onは「～を着る」という動作を表し、wearは「～を着ている」という状態を表します。

'Put on' refers to the action of putting clothes on the body. 'Wear' refers to the state of having clothes on the body.

1. **Japanese men wear black suits and white ties at weddings.**

   日本人男性は結婚式では黒のスーツに白のネクタイをします。

2. **Before the war most Japanese women wore kimonos.**

   戦前はほとんどの日本人女性は着物を着ていました。

Common Mistake 34

~~1~~ I don't want to marry with him.

~~2~~ She got married with a Frenchman.

marry や get married の後ろに with はつけません。「〜と結婚する」のように、目的語がある場合は marry を、目的語がない場合は get married を使います。

We do not use 'with' after 'marry' or 'get married'. We use 'marry' when it is followed by a direct object, and we use 'get married' when there is no direct object.

① **I don't want to marry ∧ him.**

彼と結婚したくありません。

② **She married ∧ a Frenchman.**

彼女はフランス人と結婚しました。

- I want to get married before I'm 30.
  私は30歳になる前に結婚したいです。
- Charles and Diana got married in 1981.
  チャールズとダイアナは1981年に結婚しました。

「〜と結婚する」は get married to 〜という言い方も可能ですが marry 〜のほうがふつうの言い方です。

It is possible to say 'get married to' + an object, but it is more common to say 'marry' + an object.

② **She got married to a Frenchman.**

彼女はフランス人と結婚しました。

「(〜と) 結婚している」という状態を表すときはbe married (to) です。

We can also say 'be married (to)'. This describes a state, not an action.

- She **is married to** a Frenchman.
  彼女はフランス人と結婚しています。

- My parents have **been married** for 30 years.
  私の両親は結婚して30年です。

Common Mistake 35

~~1~~ I enjoyed ∧ very much at the party.

~~2~~ We enjoyed ∧ very much.

enjoyのあとには常に目的語が必要です。目的語になるのは次の3つです。
'Enjoy' must always be followed by an object. There are three possibilities:

1. 名詞
   a noun

① **I enjoyed the party very much.**
そのパーティはとても楽しかったです。

2. 再帰代名詞（myself, ourselves, yourself, yourselves など）
   reflexive pronoun (myself, ourselves, yourself, yourselves, etc.)

① **I enjoyed myself very much at the party.**
そのパーティはとても楽しかったです。

② **We enjoyed ourselves very much.**
私たちはとても楽しかった。

3. 動名詞（-ing）
   a verb ending in '-ing'

- I enjoyed meeting him.
  彼に会って楽しかったです。
- Do you enjoy studying English?
  英語を勉強するのは楽しいですか。

Common Mistake 36

✕1 Many Japanese women retire from their jobs when they get married.

✕2 I decided to retire from the club.

retireは年をとったので退職するという意味です。再び職に就くことはないという意味合いがあるので、主に年をとった人に使う言葉です。若い人や中年の人が仕事をやめるときは、leaveやquitを使います。また「クラブをやめる」と言うときもretireでなくleaveを使います。

'Retire' means to leave one's job because one is old. It implies that one will never have another job again, so it is mainly used for old people. For young or middle-aged people, we say 'leave one's job' or 'quit one's job'. Also, we say 'leave a club' not 'retire from a club'.

① **Many Japanese women leave their jobs when they get married.**

Many Japanese women quit their jobs when they get married.

多くの日本の女性は結婚すると仕事をやめます。

② **I decided to leave the club.**

私はクラブをやめることにしました。

Common Mistake 37

✕1 I am very busy because I join a tennis club.

✕2 I met her shortly after I belonged to the tennis club.

join a clubは「クラブに入る」という動作を表し、belong to a clubは「クラブに入っている」という状態を表します。

'Join a club' means 'enter a club'. 'Belong to a club' means 'be a member of a club'.

1 **I am very busy because I belong to a tennis club.**

テニスクラブに入っているのでとても忙しいです。

2 **I met her shortly after I joined the tennis club.**

テニスクラブに入ってすぐに、彼女と知り合いました。

Common Mistake 38

✕ Midori is absent because she catches a cold.

「かぜをひく」はcatch (a) cold、「かぜをひいている」はhave a cold, have got a coldまたはhave caught (a) coldです。

'Catch (a) cold' means 'become infected with a cold'. 'Have a cold', 'have got a cold' and 'have caught (a) cold' mean 'be infected with a cold'.

◯ **Midori is absent because she has a cold.**

Midori isn't here because she's got a cold.

Midori is absent because she has caught (a) cold.

みどりさんは、かぜをひいているので欠席です。

Common Mistake 39

✕1 He is cancer.

✕2 If you smoke, you may become cancer.

だれかが「病気である」と言うときは、動詞のhaveやhave gotを使い、特定の「病気になる」と言うときはgetを使います。

We use the verbs 'have' or 'have got' to say that someone has a disease, and we use the verb 'get' to say that someone becomes ill with a particular disease.

① **He has cancer.**

He's got cancer.

彼はガンです。

② **If you smoke, you may get cancer.**

たばこを吸うと、ガンになるかもしれません。

Common Mistake 40

I took a driver's license in the vacation.

licenseは他人から与えられるので、get a licenseと言います。一般的に何かを他人から与えられるときにgetを使いますが、他人から与えられずに得る場合はtakeを使います。takeとgetについてのより詳しい説明は、よい辞書を参照してください。

We say 'get a license' because we are given it by other people. Generally speaking, we say 'get' when we are given something by another person, whereas we say 'take' if we acquire something without it being given to us. For more detailed information about 'take' and 'get', see a good dictionary.

I got a driver's license in the vacation.

私は休み中に運転免許を取りました。

- I got a letter from Rosie this morning.
  私は今朝ロージーからの手紙を受け取りました。
- It's easy to get a visa.
  ビザを取るのは簡単です。
- Someone took my umbrella.
  だれかが私の傘を持っていきました。
- He took a gun out of his pocket.
  彼はポケットの中からピストルを取り出しました。

Common Mistake 41

✗1 I love baked meat.

✗2 I baked some fish.

日本語の「焼く」という言葉はいろいろな英語になりえます。肉や魚をグリルで焼いた場合はgrillという動詞を使います。アメリカ英語ではbroilという言葉も使います。

The Japanese word *yaku* can be translated in many different ways. If meat or fish is cooked on a grill, we use the verb 'grill'. In American English one can also say 'broil'.

1 **I love grilled meat.**

私は（グリルで）焼いた肉が好きです。

2 **I grilled some fish.**

私は魚を焼きました。

bakeはパンやケーキやクッキーなどをオーブンで焼くこと、roastは大きな肉の塊をオーブンや直火で焼くこと、burnは調理しすぎて焦げることです。

'Bake' means to cook bread, cakes, cookies, etc., in an oven. 'Roast' means to cook a large piece of meat in an oven or above an open fire. 'Burn' means to cook food too much so that it becomes black.

- The oven was too hot, so the cake was burned.

  オーブンが熱すぎたので、ケーキが焦げてしまいました。

Common Mistake 42

✕1 My sister is going to bear a child soon.

✕2 She gave birth to a baby last month.

現代の日常英語ではhave a baby「出産する」という言い方をします。bear a childという表現はとても古く、今では使いませんが、I was bornという受け身の形はよく使います。give birth toという表現は、改まった、または文語的な言い方として使われます。

In modern everyday English we say 'have a baby'. The expression 'bear a child' is very old-fashioned, though we often use the passive form 'I was born'. The expression 'give birth to' is used in rather formal or literary language.

1 **My sister is going to have a baby soon.**
私の姉はもうすぐ赤ちゃんを産みます。

2 **She had a baby last month.**
彼女は先月出産しました。

Common Mistake 43

✕ I made many good memories at high school.

英語ではmake memoriesとは言いません。次のように言います。

We do not say 'make memories' in English. Instead we say the following:

I had many good experiences at high school.
高校ではたくさんよい経験をしました。

I have a lot of good memories of high school.
私には高校時代のよい思い出がたくさんあります
→ 私は高校時代によい思い出をたくさんつくりました。

Common Mistake 44

1 I have interest in European art.

2 You have much knowledge about Japan.

have interest とかhave knowledge という言い方は、ふつうはしません。「興味や知識を持っている」と言うときはbe interested あるいはknowと言います。

We usually do not say 'have interest' or 'have knowledge'. Instead we say 'be interested' or 'know'.

1 I am interested in European art.
私はヨーロッパの美術に興味があります。

2 You know a lot about Japan.
あなたは日本についての知識をたくさん持っています。

しかし、have no interest in という言い方をすることはあります。
However, we do say 'have no interest in'.

- I have no interest in phonetics.
  私は音声学には興味がありません。

Common Mistake 45

I long for France.

💡 long forは、何かを長い間とても欲しがっているという意味です。国や市など、所有できないものに対してlong forと言うことはできません。**その場合は次のように言います。**

'Long for' means to want something very much and for a long time. One cannot use 'long for' with something which cannot be owned, such as a country or city. One should say:

I long to go to France.
I'd love to go to France.
私はフランスにとても行きたい→私はフランスにあこがれています。

I'm fascinated by/with France.
私はフランスにあこがれています。

- All my life I've longed to live in Paris.
  生まれてからずっとパリに住みたいと思っています。
- I long for a house in the country with a big garden.
  私は田舎の大きな庭つきの家がとても欲しい。
- When I was a child, I longed for a pony.
  子どものとき、ポニーがとても欲しかった。

Common Mistake 46

× I wanted to go to Europe last summer, but it was too expensive, so I gave up to go.

give upの意味は、何かしていることをやめるということです。まだやり始めていないことをgive upすることはできません。**しかし、それをしようという考えをgive upすることはできます。**

'Give up' means 'stop' (doing something). If we never started doing something, we cannot say we 'gave up' doing it. However, we can say we 'gave up' the idea of doing it.

○ **I wanted to go to Europe last summer, but it was too expensive, so I changed my mind.**

I wanted to go to Europe last summer, but it was too expensive, so I gave up the idea.

昨年夏、ヨーロッパへ行こうと思いましたが、あまりに高いのでやめました。

Common Mistake 47

✕ I started associating with my boyfriend last year.

「交際する」と言いたいとき、男女間の恋愛関係に動詞associateは使いません。デートをよくするような関係はgo out togetherやgo out withなどを使って表現します。

We do not use the verb 'associate' to talk about a romantic relationship between a man and a woman. If a man and a woman are having dates together often, we say they are 'going out together' or one of them is 'going out with' the other.

○ **I started going out with my boyfriend last year.**
My boyfriend and I started going out together last year.
昨年からボーイフレンドと付き合い始めました。

動詞associateは、恋愛ではない関係に使われます。

The verb 'associate' is used to talk about non-romantic relationships.

- He **associates with** criminals.
  彼は犯罪者と付き合っています。

associateには、「頭の中で（2つの考えを）結びつける」という意味もあります。

'Associate' also means 'to connect (two ideas) in one's mind'.

- I **associate** France **with** good food.
  私はフランスといえば、おいしい料理を連想します。

Common Mistake 48

✕ My grandmother grew me up.

「育てる」はbring upです。
The Japanese word *sodateru* should be translated as 'bring up'.

My grandmother brought me up.
祖母が私を育ててくれました。

grow upは「育つ」という意味の自動詞です。
'Grow up' is an intransitive verb.

- I **grew up** in the north of England.
  私はイングランドの北部で育ちました。

Common Mistake 49

Last year I tripped to Europe.

動詞tripの意味は「つまずく」です。「旅行をする」は次のように言います。
The verb 'trip' means *tsumazuku*. One should say:

Last year I went to Europe.
去年私はヨーロッパへ行きました。

Last year I went on a trip to Europe.
去年私はヨーロッパ旅行をしました。

- I **tripped** and fell over.
  私はつまずいて転んでしまいました。

Common Mistake 50

✕1 I did homestay in America for two weeks.

I homestayed in America for two weeks.

✕2 I went to Australia for homestay.

homestay programと言うことはできますが、do homestayと言うことはできません。また、homestayを動詞として使うことはできません。次のように言うとよいでしょう。

One can say 'homestay program', but not 'do homestay'. Also, one cannot use 'homestay' as a verb. One should say:

1 **I stayed with a family in America for two weeks.**

私はアメリカで2週間ホームステイをしました。

2 **I went to Australia and stayed with an Australian family.**

私はオーストラリアへ行き、オーストラリア人の家庭にホームステイしました。

- I took part in a homestay program.

私はホームステイをしました。

Common Mistake 51

~~1~~ I've picked up five places in Europe that I want to visit.

~~2~~ The writer picked up three points in the article.

日本語の「ピックアップする」と英語のpick upは同じ意味ではありません。「いくつかある中から選ぶ」という意味の英語はpick outです。
'Pick up' does not mean the same as the Japanese *pikku appu suru*. 'Pick out' means 'choose from a group'.

① **I've picked out five places in Europe that I want to visit.**
ヨーロッパで行きたいところ5カ所をピックアップしました。

② **The writer mentioned three points in the article.**
その記者は記事で3つの点を取り上げました。

pick upには、以下のようにいくつかの意味があります。
'Pick up' has various different meanings, for example:

- He picked up the letter and opened it.
彼は手紙を拾い上げ、開封しました。
- I'll pick you up at the station.
車で駅へ迎えに行きます。
- Business is gradually picking up.
商売は徐々に景気がよくなっています。

Common Mistake 52

✗1 I challenge to learn computer programming.

✗2 I challenged the entrance examination of Tokyo University.

動詞challengeは、日本語の「チャレンジする」とは意味が違います。「チャレンジする」と言いたいときはtryを使ったほうがいいでしょう。

The verb 'challenge' does not mean the same as *charenji suru* in Japanese. It is better to say 'try'.

1. **I'm trying to learn computer programming.**
   コンピュータプログラミングの習得にチャレンジしています。
2. **I tried to pass the entrance examination of Tokyo University.**
   東大の入試にチャレンジしました。

   I tried to get into Tokyo University.
   東大にチャレンジしました。

動詞challengeは、「人に試合や戦いをいどむ」あるいは「人にとても困難なことを行うよう強く要求する」という意味です。

The verb 'challenge' means to invite someone to compete in a fight or match, or to ask someone to do something difficult.

- I challenged him to a game of tennis.
  私はテニスの試合を彼にいどみました。

仕事がchallenging（形容詞）または、a challenge（名詞）と言った場合は、「困難ではあるが、その仕事に対して意欲的である」という意味です。
If we say that a task is ‘challenging’ or ‘a challenge’, we mean that it is difficult and yet we are enthusiastic to do it.

● My new job is very **challenging**.
My new job is a real **challenge**.
私の新しい仕事は、大変ですがやりがいがあります。

Common Mistake 53

1 Hold out!

2 Do your best!

3 I want to hold out.

4 Fight!

日本語の「頑張る」とまったく同じ意味を表す英語はないので、ときどき訳すのが難しいことがあります。試験、就職の面接、試合などの緊張度の高い場面に入っていく人には、Good luck. と声をかけます。とても一生懸命働いたり、勉強したりしている人に対しては、その友人たちが Don't work too hard. とよく言います。

There is no exact equivalent for the Japanese word *ganbaru* in English, so it is sometimes difficult to translate. If someone is about to go into a stressful situation such as an examination, job interview, match, etc., we say 'Good luck' to them. If someone is working or studying very hard, their friends may say to them 'Don't work too hard'.

Good luck!

頑張って！

Don't work too hard.

頑張りすぎないでね！

「頑張りたいと思います」と言いたいときは、I'm going to do the best I can. とか I'm really going to try hard. またはアメリカ英語では I'm going to give it all I've got. と言います。

If one wants to say *ganbaritai to omoimasu*, one can say 'I'm going to do the best I can', or 'I'm really going to try hard' or, in American English, 'I'm going to give it all I've got'.

③ I'm going to do the best I can.

ベストを尽くします → 頑張りたいと思います。

I'm really going to try hard.

本当に頑張ります。

fightは「戦う」という意味なので、人が頑張るように励ますときに、この言葉は使いません。この場合もまた、Good luck!が一番よい言い方です。
'Fight' means *tatakau*, so we do not use it to encourage someone to make an effort. Again, the best thing to say is 'Good luck!'

④ Good luck!

頑張って！

Common Mistake 54

✕1 English people are drinking a lot of tea.

✕2 Every summer many Japanese people are going back to their hometown.

くり返し起こる動作について話すときは、現在時制が使われます。
The simple present tense is used to talk about actions which happen repeatedly.

1 **English people drink a lot of tea.**
イギリス人は紅茶をたくさん飲みます。

2 **Every summer many Japanese people go back to their hometown.**
毎年夏になると大勢の日本人がふるさとへ帰ります。

現在進行形が使われるのは、次のような場合です。
The present continuous tense is used as follows.

1. 話している瞬間に起こっている動作について述べるとき
For an action happening now, at the moment of speaking.
   - The kettle's **boiling**.
   やかんの湯が煮立っています。
   - It's **raining**.
   雨が降っています。

2. 一時的な状態について述べるとき
For a temporary situation.
   - I'm **staying** with a friend at the moment.
   今、私は友人のところに滞在しています。
   - I'm **working** as a waitress for a few months.
   私はここ数カ月ウェイトレスとして働いています。

3. 次第に変化している状態について述べるとき
For a gradually changing situation.

- The number of unemployed people **is increasing**.
  失業者の数**が増加しています**。

- Venice **is** gradually **sinking** into the sea.
  ベニスは次第に海に**沈んでいっています**。

4. 頻繁にくり返されること、特にそれによって話し手がイライラしていることを述べるとき。この表現にはalwaysが入ります。
With 'always' for a frequently repeated action, especially if it annoys the speaker.

- **I'm always forgetting** people's names.
  どうも人の名前**を忘れてばかりいます**。

- He**'s always asking** me to lend him money.
  彼は**いつも**お金を貸してくれと**頼んできます**。

Common Mistake 55

✗1 I was living in America for five years when I was a child.

✗2 We were waiting for an hour, and then we left.

過去の終わった動作については、たとえ、動作の継続について言う場合でも、ふつうは過去時制を使います。

We usually use the simple past tense to talk about completed past actions, even when we are talking about the duration of an action.

① **I lived in America for five years when I was a child.**

子どものころアメリカに5年間住んでいました。

② **We waited for an hour, and then we left.**

私たちは1時間待って、そこを離れました。

過去進行形は、過去のある時点で起こっていたことを伝えるときに使います。

We use the past continuous tense ('was living') to talk about what was already happening at a particular past moment.

- I was living in America when the war broke out.
  戦争が始まったとき、私はアメリカに住んでいました。
- It was raining at 6 o'clock this morning.
  今朝6時に雨が降っていました。

Common Mistake 56

Last year I had stayed in Beijing for ten days.

Last year I had been staying in Beijing for ten days.

過去の終わった動作については、たとえ、動作の継続について言う場合でも、ふつうは過去時制を使います。

We usually use the simple past tense for completed past actions, even when we are talking about the duration of an action.

Last year I stayed in Beijing for ten days.

去年、北京に10日間滞在しました。

過去完了形は、過去のある出来事が、もう1つ別の過去の出来事よりも前に起こったということを強調したいときに使います。

We use the past perfect tense ('had gone') when we want to emphasize that one past action happened before another past action.

- When I arrived at the station, the train had left.
  駅に着いたとき、列車はすでに出発してしまっていました。
- I felt ill because I had eaten too much.
  食べすぎたので、気分が悪かった。

Common Mistake 57

✗1 Japan became rich since the Second World War.

✗2 I made many new friends this year.

過去に始まり現在も続いている動作や状況について話すときは、現在完了時制を使います。

We use the present perfect tense ('has become') to talk about actions and situations which started in the past and have continued up to the present time. Thus, one should say:

1 **Japan has become rich since the Second World War.**

日本は第二次世界大戦のあと、富める国になりました。

日本は今も富める国なので、現在完了を使います。

Japan is rich now, so we use the present perfect.

2 **I have made many new friends this year.**

今年はたくさんの友達ができました。

「今年」はまだ終わっていないし、今でも友達だと思われるので現在完了を使います。

This year has not ended yet, and presumably the speaker still has his/her new friends.

Common Mistake 58

A: What are you going to do in the vacation?

B: I don't decide.

「まだ決めていない」はI haven't decided (yet)です。

One should say:

A: What are you going to do in the vacation?

休みには何をするのですか。

B: I haven't decided.

まだ決めていません。

Common Mistake 59

✗1 I could get my driver's license this summer.

✗2 I could make many friends this summer.

過去のある特定のときにできたことを表現するときは、couldではなくwas able toを使います。それが難しくて努力が必要だった場合はmanaged toを使います。

We do not use 'could' to say that we were able to do something at one particular time in the past. Instead we say 'was able to' or, if the task was difficult and required effort, 'managed to'.

1 **I was able to get my driver's license this summer.**

今年の夏、私は運転免許が取れました。

I managed to get my driver's license this summer.

今年の夏、私はどうにか運転免許が取れました。

あるいは、過去形を使うこともできます。

Alternatively, we can use the simple past tense.

1 **I got my driver's license this summer.**

今年の夏、私は運転免許を取りました。

2 **I made many friends this summer.**

今年の夏は友達がたくさんできました。

couldは、過去にやろうと思えばいつでもできたことを表現するときに使います。

'Could' is used to say that one could do something any time one wanted to.

- The house was by the sea so we **could go swimming** whenever we wanted to.
  その家は海の近くだったので、私たちはいつでも好きなときに泳ぎに行けました。
- My grandfather **could speak** five languages.
  祖父は5カ国語を話せました。

「過去のある特定のときにできたこと」の場合でも、知覚動詞（see, hear, feelなど）の前ではcouldを使うことができます。

We can also use 'could' with verbs of perception, such as 'see', 'hear', 'feel', etc., even when we are talking about a particular time.

- When the mist cleared, we **could see** Mount Fuji.
  霧が晴れると、富士山が見えました。

could notはどんな状況でも使えます。

'Could not' can be used in any situation.

- I **couldn't go** to the party on Christmas Eve.
  クリスマスイブのパーティに行けませんでした。

Common Mistake 60

× *A*: What will you do at [on] the weekend?
B: I will play tennis with Tim on Sunday.

会話では、はっきり決まっている予定や、話しているときより前に決めた意図について話すときは、willではなくbe going toを使います。
In conversation, we use 'going to', not 'will' to talk about definite future plans and intentions which have been made before the moment of speaking.

○ ***A*: What are you going to do at [on] the weekend?**
今度の週末は何をしますか。

***B*: I'm going to play tennis with Tim on Sunday.**
日曜日にティムとテニスをします。

はっきり決まっている予定や計画について話すとき、いつのことなのか「時」について述べれば、現在進行形を使うこともできます。その計画に2人以上の人がかかわっている場合、特にその傾向があります。
If we mention a time, we can also use the present continuous tense to talk about definite future plans and arrangements, especially if the plans involve more than one person.

○ ***A*: What are you doing at [on] the weekend?**
***B*: I'm playing tennis with Tim on Sunday.**

はっきり決まっている予定や、話すとき以前に決めた意図以外で未来について話すときは、willを使います。

We use ‘will’ when we are talking about the future, with the exception of definite plans and intentions made before the moment of speaking.

- My father **will be** 65 in September.
  父は9月に65歳になります。
- I think it’**ll rain** this afternoon.
  今日の午後は雨になるでしょう。

上の2つの文は、予定でも意図でもないのでwillが使われています。

In the two sentences above, ‘will’ is used because the speaker is not talking about a plan or intention.

- I think I’**ll stay** at home this evening.
  今日の夕方は家にいると思います。
- *A*: Can someone help me?
  だれか手伝ってくれますか。
  B: Yes, I **will**.
  ええ、手伝いますよ。

上の1つ目の文は、あまりはっきりしない意図について話しているのでwillが使われています。2つ目の文は、話す瞬間に決まった意図なのでwillが使われています。

In the first sentence, ‘will’ is used because the speaker is expressing an intention which is not definite. In the second sentence, ‘will’ is used because the speaker is expressing an intention which he/she made at the moment of speaking.

Common Mistake 61

✗1 I was stolen my bicycle.

✗2 I was taken my photograph wearing a kimono.

英語でこういう型式の文章を使うことはできません。この場合は、《主語＋have＋目的語＋過去分詞》の形を用います。
This type of sentence is impossible in English. One should use the following structure: subject + ‘have’ + object + past participle.

① **I had my bicycle stolen.**
私は自転車を盗まれました。

② **I had my photograph taken wearing a kimono.**
私は着物を着て写真を撮ってもらいました。

あるいは、受動態で表現することもできます。
Alternatively, one can use the passive.

① **My bicycle was stolen.**

Common Mistake 62

 I was got angry by my father.

「～に怒られた」と言いたいとき、get angry を受動態にすることはできません。**次のように言います。**

It is not possible to make a passive of 'get angry'. One should say:

 **My father got angry with me.**

My father got mad at me.（アメリカ英語）

父は私に怒った → 私は父に怒られた。

現代の英語では、scold（叱る）はあまり使われません。

In modern English, the word 'scold' is not common.

Common Mistake 63

 1 To drink too much is bad for one's health.

 2 I think to live in a foreign country is very interesting.

古い英語では、不定詞（to＋動詞の原形）を文や節の初めに置いて、主語として使うことがよくありましたが、現代の英語では、ふつう、動名詞（動詞の -ing形）が用いられます。

In older English, the infinitive was often used as the subject at the beginning of a sentence or clause. In modern English, however, we usually use the gerund (verb + '-ing') instead.

① **Drinking too much is bad for one's health.**

飲みすぎは健康によくありません。

② **I think living in a foreign country is very interesting.**

外国で生活をすることはとてもおもしろいと思います。

また、itを文や節の初めに置き、あとで不定詞を使うこともできます。

Alternatively, we can begin the sentence or clause with 'it' and put the infinitive later in the sentence or clause.

① **It is bad for one's health to drink too much.**

② **I think it is very interesting to live in a foreign country.**

1つの特定の動作を言うときは、動名詞より《it＋to不定詞》の形を使うほうが一般的です。

If we are talking about one particular action, the structure with 'it' and a to-infinitive is more common than the gerund.

- It's nice to see you again.

  またお目にかかれてうれしいです。

この場合Seeing you again is nice.とは言えません。

Not *Seeing you again is nice.

Common Mistake 64

How to study in British universities is different from Japan.

《how to＋動詞の原形》は、ふつうは文や節の主語として使うことはできません。次のように表します。

The expression 'how to' + infinitive is not usually used as the subject of a sentence or clause. One should say:

The way of studying in British universities is different from Japan.

イギリスの大学の勉強方法は日本とは違います。

《how to＋動詞の原形》は、知ることや学ぶことに関係ある動詞（know, understand, learn, discover, teach, explain, show, tell, askなど）のあとで使います。

'How to' + infinitive is used after verbs related to knowledge and learning, i.e. 'know', 'understand', 'learn', 'discover', 'teach', 'explain', 'show', 'tell', 'ask', etc.

- Do you know **how to make** pancakes?
  パンケーキの作り方を知っていますか。
- My brother taught me **how to drive**.
  兄が運転を教えてくれました。

説明書にも使われます。

It can also be used in written instructions.

- **How to use** the water heater: first, press the red button, then ...
  湯沸かし器の使い方：最初に赤いボタンを押し、次に…。

Common Mistake 65

✗1 I stopped to smoke two years ago.

✗2 We stopped to see each other when I moved to Osaka.

《stop＋to不定詞》の意味は、「ほかのことをするために、何かをするのをやめる」ということです。《stop＋動詞のing形》の意味は、「～するのをやめる」です。

'Stop' followed by a to-infinitive means to stop doing something in order to do something else. 'Stop' followed by a verb ending in '-ing' means *suru no o yameru.*

1. **I stopped smoking two years ago.**
   私は2年前にたばこを吸うのをやめました。
2. **We stopped seeing each other when I moved to Osaka.**
   私が大阪に引っ越したときに、私たちは会うのをやめました。

- We started work at 9 o'clock, and then stopped to have tea at 10:30.
  私たちは9時に仕事を始め、その後10時半に中断してお茶にしました。
- We stopped to look at the view.
  私たちは景色を見るために立ち止まりました。

《stop＋動詞のing形》のほうが《stop＋to不定詞》よりも、はるかによく使われる形です。

'Stop' followed by a verb ending in '-ing' is much more common than 'stop' followed by a to-infinitive.

Common Mistake 66

✕1 If I have a lot of money, I ∧ travel all over the world.

✕2 If I am rich, I ∧ buy a house in Hawaii.

✕3 If I am a vegetarian, it is difficult to eat in restaurants.

✕4 If I have a car, I can come here in 20 minutes.

✕5 If I stop working, I can't live.

現在または未来における想像上のような非現実的な状況を述べる場合は、if節に過去時制、主節にはwould＋（toのない）不定詞を用います。この構造は主に、起こりそうもないと思われることに使います。if節ではwasの代わりにwereがよく使われます。

When we talk about an imaginary, unreal situation in the present or future, we use the past tense in the if-clause, and we use 'would' plus the infinitive in the main clause. We use this structure mainly for situations which we think are unlikely to happen. 'Were' is often used instead of 'was' in the if-clause.

① **If I had a lot of money, I would travel all over the world.**

お金をたくさん持っていたら、世界中を旅します。

② **If I were rich, I would buy a house in Hawaii.**

お金持ちだったら、ハワイに家を買うでしょう。

3 動詞に関する間違い

③ **If I were a vegetarian, it would be difficult to eat in restaurants.**

もし私がベジタリアンだったら、レストランで食べるのは難しいでしょう。

「～できるだろうに」の意味では、主節のwouldの代わりにcouldを使います。

We use 'could' instead of 'would' in the main clause to mean 'would be able to'.

④ **If I had a car, I could come here in 20 minutes.**

車があれば20分でここに来られるでしょう。

⑤ **If I stopped working, I couldn't live.**

働くのをやめたら、生きていけないでしょう。

実際には起こらなかった過去の状況を述べる場合は、if節に過去完了時制（had＋過去分詞）を、主節には《would/could have＋過去分詞》を用います。

When we talk about an imaginary situation in the past, we use the past perfect tense (for example, 'had done') in the if-clause, and we use 'would have' or 'could have' in the main clause.

- If Trump **had lost** the election in 2016, Hillary Clinton **would have become** president.

  トランプが2016年の選挙に敗れていたら、ヒラリー・クリントンが大統領になっていたでしょう。

- If I **hadn't been late** for the interview, I **could have got** the job.

  面接に遅刻していなかったら、その仕事を得ていたでしょうに。

Exercise 3

次の文中の間違いを見つけて正しい英語に直してください。文末のかっこ内の数は、間違いの数を示しています。答えは巻末にあります。

1. I will meet my friend at 7 o'clock this evening and we will see movie. (3)

2. I was living in London from 1979 to 1981 (1)

3. I had gone to Nagano last week. (1)

4. Japan changed very much since the war. (1)

5. She was stolen her purse. (1)

6. I join the baseball club since April. (2)

7. I became to like studying English. (1)

8. She married with foreigner. (2)

9. I enjoyed very much. (1)

10. I wish you are successful. (1)

11. Every autumn the leaves are turning red. (1)

✎ ______________________________

12. Japanese businessman has no time to play. (3)

✎ ______________________________

13. My grandfather was dead in the war. (1)

✎ ______________________________

14. Please teach me your address. (1)

✎ ______________________________

15. I have many happy memories when I watch the photographs of last summer. (1)

✎ ______________________________

16. She presented me some chocolate on Valentine's Day. (1)

✎ ______________________________

17. It costs a lot of money to borrow wedding kimono. (2)

✎ ______________________________

18. When I was child, I liked writing picture. (3)

✎ ______________________________

19. I challenge to learn German. (1)

✎ ______________________________

20. After climbing for four hours, we could reach the top of mountain. (2)

✎ ______________________________

21. I started playing judo when I was junior high school student. (2)

____

22. I knew many interesting things by talking with him. (1)

____

23. She retired from her job in order to have a baby. (1)

____

24. I put on black kimono at the funeral. (2)

____

25. I don't feel well because I catch a cold. (1)

____

26. He escaped from home when he was teenager. (2)

____

27. I am often said that I look very young. (1)

____

28. My car slipped on some ice. (1)

____

29. I have associated with my girlfriend for two years. (1)

____

30. I've picked up the three most important points in this book. (1)

____

31. I wanted to go on a trip with my boyfriend, but my parents didn't admit me. (1)

32. Our team won the other team. (1)

33. To speak Chinese is very difficult. (1)

34. The job doesn't fit me. (1)

35. John Lennon was grown up by his aunt. (1)

36. I was got angry by my mother. (1)

37. If I am man, I can get higher salary. (4)

38. I want to take driver's license. (2)

39. She bore a baby recently. (1)

40. *Yakitori* means 'baked chicken'. (1)

41. I made many good memories in Australia. (2)

✎ ______________________________

42. The food we eat includes a lot of sugar and chemicals. (1)

✎ ______________________________

43. I tripped to Hawaii. (1)

✎ ______________________________

44. He is AIDS. (1)

✎ ______________________________

45. I stopped to smoke because I don't want to be cancer. (2)

✎ ______________________________

46. I long for Europe. (1)

✎ ______________________________

47. I homestayed in New Zealand. (1)

✎ ______________________________

48. Studying Chinese is difficult, but I will hold out. (1)

✎ ______________________________

49. He said 'Fight!' to me before the exam. (1)

✎ ______________________________

50. I have interest in European culture. (1)

✎ ______________________________

51. I don't decide what I am going to do. (1)

✎ ______________________________

Chapter 4

形容詞・副詞に関する間違い

Problems with Adjectives and Adverbs

Common Mistake 67

✕1 My salary is cheap.

✕2 I like the job but the pay is very cheap.

給料や賃金が安いと言うときは、cheapではなくlowを使います。**cheapは値段が安いと言うときに使う言葉です。**

We use 'low', not 'cheap', to describe a salary or pay. 'Cheap' is used to describe prices.

1 **My salary is low.**

私の給料は安い。

2 **I like the job but the pay is very low.**

その仕事は好きですが、給料がすごく安いです。

Common Mistake 68

✗1 Tokyo is very wide.

✗2 There are seven people living in my house, so it is very narrow.

wideやnarrowは大きさではなく、幅が「広い」「狭い」と言うときに使う言葉です。**例えばa wide road, a wide river, a narrow streetなどです。**大きさを表すにはbig, large, smallを使います。十分なスペースがないという意味の「狭い」はcrampedです。

'Wide' and 'narrow' are used to describe width, not size, for example 'a wide road', 'a wide river', 'a narrow street', etc. We use 'big', 'large' and 'small' to describe size. We say 'cramped' if there is not enough space.

1 **Tokyo is very big.**

東京はとても広い。

2 **There are seven people living in my house, so it is very cramped.**

わが家には7人が住んでいるので、とても狭いです。

Common Mistake 69

✕1 I think my boyfriend is very pretty.

✕2 My dog is very pretty.

pretty という語は、若い女性や少女、小さな子ども、また女性的なものや小さなもの（例えばドレス、花、小さな庭など）を表すときに使います。**男性や動物を表すときは使いません。**

'Pretty' is used to describe young women, girls, little children and things which are feminine and/or small, i.e. a dress, a flower, a small garden, etc. We do not use it to describe men or animals.

1 **I think my boyfriend is very good-looking/handsome/cute.**

私のボーイフレンドは美男子だ［ハンサムだ、かわいい］と思います。

2 **My dog is very cute.**

My dog is very sweet.（特にイギリス英語）

私の犬はとてもかわいい。

Common Mistake 70

~~1~~ Skiing is very interesting.

~~2~~ The movie was very interesting, so we laughed a lot.

何かがinterestingだと言ったら、それは思考や知性の関心を引き起こすという意味です。特に知的ではないけれども楽しいこと（スポーツ、パーティ、旅行など）には、funやenjoyableを使います。笑わせられるものにはfunnyを使います。

If we say that something is 'interesting', we mean that it interests our mind and intellect. If something gives us pleasure which is not primarily intellectual, for example, a sport, party, trip, etc., we say that it is 'fun' or 'enjoyable'. If something makes us laugh, we say that it is 'funny'.

1 **Skiing is a lot of fun.**

Skiing is really fun.

スキーはとてもおもしろい。

2 **The movie was very funny, so we laughed a lot.**

その映画はおかしくて私たちは大笑いをしました。

Common Mistake 71

✕ My four-year-old nephew is very wise.

wiseは判断力に優れ正しい決断ができるという意味です。「人がwiseである」と言ったら、その人が成熟していて経験が豊富であるという意味合いが含まれているので、子どもについて表すときにwiseという語はめったに使いません。物覚えが速く理解力があるという意味で「賢い」と言いたいときは、cleverやintelligentを使います。

'Wise' means 'having good judgment and making good decisions'. If we say someone is wise, we imply that they are mature and experienced, so the word is rarely used to describe a child. If we want to say that someone is quick at learning and understanding, we use the words 'clever' or 'intelligent'.

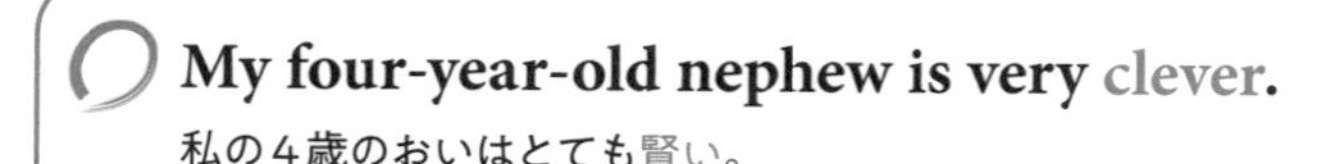

My four-year-old nephew is very clever.

私の4歳のおいはとても賢い。

Common Mistake 72

✕ 1 I always feel ashamed when I have to give a speech.

✕ 2 This morning I said 'Hello' to a man in the street who looked like my friend, but in fact he was a stranger, so I felt very ashamed.

人前で話したり歌ったりしなければならないときや、ばかげた失敗をしたときに恥ずかしいと思うのは、ashamedではなくembarrassedです。

There is a difference between 'embarrassed' and 'ashamed'. People feel 'embarrassed', not 'ashamed', when they have to give a speech or sing in front of other people, or if they make a silly mistake in front of other people.

1 I always feel embarrassed when I have to give a speech.

スピーチをするとき、いつも恥ずかしく思います。

2 This morning I said 'Hello' to a man in the street who looked like my friend, but in fact he was a stranger, so I felt very embarrassed.

今朝友達によく似ている人に道端で「こんにちは」と言ったら人違いで、とてもきまりが悪かったです。

よくない行い（例えばうそをつく、窃盗など）をしたり、何かが不十分で恥ずかしいと思う、と言うときはashamedです。

People feel ashamed if they have done something bad, or if they feel inadequate in some way.

- I was ashamed that I had lied.
  うそをついたのが恥ずかしかったです。
- He is very ashamed of his bad handwriting.
  彼は字が下手なのをとても恥じています。

Common Mistake 73

✕1 I'm absorbed in computers.

✕2 My brother is absorbed in soccer.

人が何かに熱心で、長い時間をそれに費やしているときは、He/She is really into ～と言います。この表現はくだけた話し言葉でとてもよく使われます。また、He/She is crazy about ～, He/She loves ～, He/She is really keen on ～と言うこともできます。

If someone is very keen about something and spends a lot of time doing it, we say 'he/she is really into ～ '. This expression is informal and colloquial, and very common. We can also say 'he/she is crazy about ～' or 'he/she loves ～' or 'he/she is really keen on ～'.

1 **I'm really into computers.**

I love computers.

私はコンピュータに夢中です。

2 **My brother is really into soccer.**

My brother is crazy about soccer.

My brother is really keen on soccer.

兄はサッカーに夢中です。

《人 is absorbed in something》と言ったら、ある特定の瞬間に、その人がすべての注意を何かに注いでいるという意味です。

If we say that someone is 'absorbed' in something, it means that they are giving all of their attention to something at a particular moment.

- I was so absorbed in a book that I didn't hear him come in.

  本に夢中だったので、私は彼が入ってくるのが聞こえませんでした。

Common Mistake 74

✗1 I'm exciting because I'm going to meet my girlfriend this evening.

✗2 I always feel boring and sleepy in Mr. Webb's lessons.

✗3 His lessons are bored.

人の感情を表すには、excited, bored, moved, tired, interested, worried, frightenedなどの過去分詞（動詞＋-ed）を使います。

We use the following past participles (ending in '-ed') to say how we feel: 'excited', 'bored', 'moved', 'tired', 'interested', 'worried', 'frightened', etc.

1 **I'm excited because I'm going to meet my girlfriend this evening.**

今晩ガールフレンドに会うことになっているので、わくわくしています。

2 **I always feel bored and sleepy in Mr. Webb's lessons.**

ウェブ先生の授業はいつも退屈で眠くなります。

- I was very moved at the end of the movie.

その映画の最後でとても感動しました。

いろいろな感情を起こさせる物や人を表すには、exciting, boring, moving, tiringなどの現在分詞（動詞＋-ing）を使います。

We use the present participles 'exciting', 'boring', 'moving', 'tiring', etc. (ending in '-ing') to describe the thing or person that makes us feel excited, bored, moved, tired, etc.

3 His lessons are boring.
彼の授業は退屈です。

- He is a **boring** teacher.
  彼は退屈な先生です。
- The match was very **exciting**.
  その試合は、はらはらしておもしろかったです。
- The film was very **moving**.
  その映画はとても感動的でした。

Common Mistake 75

~~1~~ I was very terrible in the earthquake.

I was very fearful in the earthquake.

~~2~~ My father is very terrible when he gets angry.

恐怖感を表すにはfrightenedやscared, terrified, afraidの形容詞を使います。この中でterrifiedが一番強い表現です。fearfulは現代の日常英語ではあまり使いません。
We use the adjectives 'frightened', 'scared', 'terrified' and 'afraid' to talk about feelings of fear. 'Terrified' is the strongest of these adjectives. The word 'fearful' is not common in modern everyday English.

1 I was very frightened in the earthquake.
I was terrified in the earthquake.
地震のときとてもこわかったです。

恐怖感を起こさせる物や人を表すには、frighteningやscary, terrifyingの形容詞を使います。**この中でterrifyingが一番強い表現です。**

We use the adjectives ‘frightening’, ‘scary’ and ‘terrifying’ to describe something or someone who makes us feel frightened. ‘Terrifying’ is the strongest of these adjectives.

My father is very frightening when he gets angry.

父は怒るととてもこわい。

- The earthquake was **terrifying**.
  地震は恐ろしかったです。

現代英語でのterribleは一般的に「とても悪い」という意味です。

In modern English ‘terrible’ usually means ‘very bad’.

- The food was **terrible**.
  食事はとてもまずかったです。
- The weather was **terrible**.
  天気はひどかったです。
- I’m **terrible** at singing.
  私は歌がとても下手です。

Common Mistake 76

✗1 I was very painful.

✗2 I felt very painful.

「人is painful」または「人feels painful」と言うことはできません。「痛い」と言いたいときは次のように表します。
We cannot say that a person 'is painful' or 'feels painful'. We should say:

1. **I was in great pain/in a lot of pain.**
   とても痛かったです。
2. **I felt a lot of pain.**
   とても痛かったです。

「傷や体の一部分is painful」と言うことはできます。また「経験や記憶is painful」とも言えます。
We say that a wound or a part of the body is 'painful'. We can also say that an experience or memory is 'painful'.

- My leg was very painful.
  脚がとても痛かった。
- Saying goodbye to her was very painful.
  彼女にさよならを言うのはとてもつらかった。

Common Mistake 77

 I was very enjoyable.

「人 is enjoyable」と言うことはできません。enjoyableは経験、パーティ、旅行、休暇など、人に楽しみを与えるものを表すときに使います。「私は楽しかった」と言いたいときは、次のように表現します。

We cannot say that a person is 'enjoyable'. 'Enjoyable' is used to describe things which give a person enjoyment, such as an experience, a party, a trip, a holiday, etc.

 **I enjoyed myself very much.**

私はとても楽しかった。

I had a very enjoyable time.

とても楽しい時を過ごしました。

● The party was very **enjoyable**.

パーティはとても楽しかった。

Common Mistake 78

✗1 I am very hard to get up at 6 a.m.

✗2 I am easy to get depressed.

✗3 He is easy to get angry.

「～するのは私にとって難しい」と言うときはI am hard toではなく、次のように言います。

One cannot say 'I am hard to' when one means 'I have difficulty doing something'. One should say:

① **Getting up at 6 a.m. is very hard for me.**

I find getting up at 6 a.m. very hard.

I find it very hard to get up at 6 a.m.

I have difficulty getting up at 6 a.m.

朝6時に起きるのは私にはとても大変です。

また、「私は簡単に～する」「～しやすい」はI am easy toではなく、次のように言います。

Also, one cannot say 'I am easy to' when one means 'I do something with ease'. One should say:

② **I get depressed easily.**

私は簡単に落ち込んでしまいます。

③ **He gets angry easily.**

彼はすぐ怒ります。

《主語＋be hard (easy)＋to不定詞》の形の文で、beの主語と不定詞の主語は同一ではありません。

In the structure subject + 'be hard (easy)' + to-infinitive, the subject of 'be' is not the same as the subject of the infinitive.

- His English **is hard to** understand. (= I have difficulty understanding his English.)
  彼の英語はわかりにくい。
- My computer **is** really **easy to** use. (= I can use my computer with ease.)
  私のコンピュータはとても使いやすい。
- It's so **easy to** fall in love. (= People fall in love easily.)
  恋に落ちるのは簡単です。

Common Mistake 79

✕ She's half.

日本人と外国人との間に生まれた人を表すのに、She's half と言うことはできません。次のように言います。

One cannot say 'She's half' to describe a person who has one Japanese parent and one non-Japanese parent. One should say:

She's half-Japanese.
彼女はハーフです。

Her father is American and her mother is Japanese.
彼女のお父さんはアメリカ人で、お母さんは日本人です → 彼女はハーフです。

She's Japanese-American.
彼女は日系アメリカ人です。

Common Mistake 80

✕1 Every people in this company works too hard.

✕2 Every children in the school liked her.

✕3 All people in Japan are very busy.

everyは常に単数形の名詞と一緒に使い、複数名詞と一緒に用いられることはありません。people, childrenは複数名詞なので、「すべての～」と言いたいときは、それぞれeveryone/everybody, every child/all (the) childrenと言います。

'Every' is used with singular countable nouns. It cannot be used with plural nouns such as 'people' or 'children'. We should say 'everyone', or 'everybody', 'every child' or 'all (the) children'.

1 **Everyone in this company works too hard.**
この会社の人はみんな働きすぎます。

2 **Every child in the school liked her.**
その学校のどの子どもも彼女が好きでした。

All the children in the school liked her.
その学校の子どもはみんな彼女が好きでした。

ふつうall peopleとは言えませんが、all Japanese peopleとかall the people in the roomなどのように、all ～ peopleと言うことはできます。

Also, it is unusual to say 'all people', though we can say 'all Japanese people' and 'all the people in the room'.

All Japanese people are very busy.

Everyone in Japan is very busy.

日本の人はみんな忙しい。

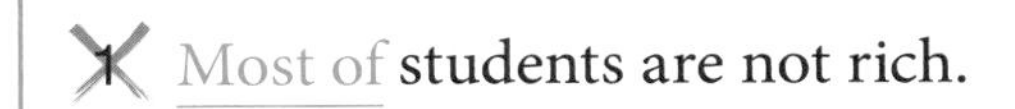

Common Mistake 81

~~1~~ Most of students are not rich.

~~2~~ Almost Japanese are afraid of earthquakes.

~~3~~ Almost my friends are women.

「ほとんどの～」と言いたいとき、「the, this, that, these, those」、「代名詞」、「所有形容詞（my, your, hisなど）」、「固有名詞」の前では、most ofが使われます。**しかし、これらがないときはofなしでmostだけを使います。**

'Most of' is used before 'the', 'this', 'that', 'these', 'those', pronouns, possessive adjectives ('my', 'your', 'his', etc.) and proper nouns. If there is not one of these words, we use 'most' without 'of'.

Most ∧ students are not rich.

ほとんどの学生は金持ちではありません。

- Most of the people I met in China were very kind.
  中国で私が会ったほとんどの人はとても親切でした。
- I've read most of Mishima's novels.
  私は三島のほとんどの小説を読みました。

almostは副詞です。**名詞の前で「ほとんどの～」という意味では使えません。**

'Almost' is an adverb. It is not used before nouns to mean 'most'.

② **Most Japanese are afraid of earthquakes.**
ほとんどの日本人は地震をこわがっています。

③ **Most of my friends are women.**
私の友達はほとんど女性です。

- I **almost** died.
  私はもう少しで死ぬところでした。
- It's **almost** five o'clock.
  もうすぐ5時です。

almost all と most (of) はまったく同じ意味ではありません。almost all は99%ぐらいを表すのに対し、most (of) は50%以上を表しています。
'Almost all' is not exactly the same as 'most (of)'. 'Almost all' means something like 99%, whereas 'most (of)' means more than 50%.

- **Almost all** Japanese people are afraid of earthquakes.
  ほぼすべての日本人が地震をこわがっています。

Common Mistake 82

✗1 In Tokyo foreigners are many.

✗2 In my hometown foreigners are few.

✗3 During the war food was little.

次の文型は、文語的表現としてたまに使われますが、日常の英語では使いません。

1) 主語＋are many
2) 主語＋are few
3) 主語＋is much
4) 主語＋is little（量を表すとき）

日常の英語では、次のような文型を使います。

1) There are a lot of/lots of/many＋複数名詞
2) There are very few/not many＋複数名詞
3) There is a lot of/lots of＋数えられない名詞
4) There is very little/not much＋数えられない名詞

この文型ではふつう、fewとlittleの前にveryをつけることに注意してください。

The following structures are not used in everyday English, though they are occasionally used in a literary style:

1) subject + 'are many'
2) subject + 'are few'
3) subject + 'is much'
4) subject + 'is little'

In everyday English we say:

1) 'There are a lot of/lots of/many' + plural noun
2) 'There are very few/not many' + plural noun
3) 'There is a lot of/lots of' + uncountable noun
4) 'There is very little/not much' + uncountable noun

Note that we usually put 'very' before 'few' and 'little' in this structure.

1. **There are lots of foreigners in Tokyo.**
   東京には外国人が多い。
2. **There are very few foreigners in my hometown.**
   私の故郷には外国人はとても少ない。
3. **There was very little food during the war.**
   戦争中、食物がとても少なかった。

littleが量でなく、大きさを表すときは《主語＋be little》と言うことができます。

We can say subject + ‘be little’ when ‘little’ refers to size, not quantity.

- My grandmother is very little.
  私の祖母はとても小柄だ。

Common Mistake 83

✕1 I spent much money.

✕2 We drank much beer.

✕3 She talks much.

形式にこだわらない日常英語では、肯定文ではふつうmuchよりa lot (of)やlots (of) を使います。a lot (of) とlots (of) は同じ意味です。

In informal, everyday English we usually say 'a lot (of)' or 'lots (of)' rather than 'much' in affirmative sentences. 'A lot (of)' and 'lots (of)' mean the same.

1. **I spent a lot of money.**
   たくさんお金を使いました。
2. **We drank lots of beer.**
   私たちはビールをたくさん飲みました。
3. **She talks a lot.**
   彼女はよくしゃべります。

muchは、疑問文や否定文で使います。また、too、so、asの後ろにもmuchを使います。

We use 'much' in questions and negative sentences. We also use 'much' after 'too', 'so' and 'as'.

- Did you spend much money?
  たくさんお金を使いましたか。
- I didn't drink much beer.
  ビールはたくさんは飲みませんでした。
- She talks too much.
  彼女はしゃべりすぎです。

● Eat as **much** as you want.
好きなだけおあがりなさい。

🔍 much は too の前や比較級の形容詞（bigger、better、more interesting など）の前でも使います。
We also use 'much' before 'too' and before comparative adjectives (i.e. 'bigger', 'better', 'more interesting', etc.).

● It's **much** too hot to study today.
今日は暑すぎて勉強できません。

● Tokyo is **much** bigger than Kyoto.
東京は京都よりずっと広い。

🔍 肯定文中の like, love, enjoy, admire, respect, thank you のあとには、よく very much をつけます。
We often say 'very much' after 'like', 'love', 'enjoy', 'admire', 'respect' and 'thank you' in affirmative sentences.

● I like you **very much**.
私はあなたがとても好きです。

● We enjoyed the trip **very much**.
私たちは旅行をとても楽しみました。

🔍 少し形式ばった言い方では、肯定文でよく much が使われます。
In more formal English, 'much' is often used in affirmative sentences.

● **Much** has been said about the dangers of pollution.
公害の危険性について多くのことが議論されています。

🔍 形式にこだわらない話し言葉では、many を much と同様に使います。つまり、「疑問文中」、「否定文中」、「too, so, as の後ろ」でのみ使われます。肯定文では many の代わりに a lot (of) や lots (of) を使います。しかし書き言葉では、肯定文中でもしばしば many が使われます。
In informal spoken English, 'many' is used in the same way as 'much', i.e. it is only used in questions, negative sentences and after 'too', 'so' and 'as'. In affirmative sentences, 'a lot (of)' or 'lots (of)' are used instead. However, in written English 'many' is often used in affirmative sentences.

● I met many interesting people. (written English)
私は多くの興味深い人たちに会いました。〈書き言葉〉

● I met lots of interesting people. (colloquial English)
私は多くの興味深い人たちに会いました。〈話し言葉〉

Common Mistake 84

✕1 The food was very terrible.

✕2 The weather was very wonderful.

✕3 They live in a very enormous house.

次にあげる極度の性質を表す形容詞の前には、ふつうveryをつけません。terrible, awful, wonderful, excellent, marvelous, enormous, huge, massive, tiny, exhausted, astonished, amazed, delighted, miserable, gorgeous, extraordinaryなどです。例えばterribleは、これ以上悪くできないほどとても悪いという意味なので、veryをつけても意味を強めることはできないからです。しかしreallyやabsolutelyをつけることはできます。

We do not usually use 'very' with adjectives which describe some extreme quality, for example 'terrible', 'awful', 'wonderful', 'excellent', 'marvelous', 'enormous', 'huge', 'massive', 'tiny', 'exhausted', 'astonished', 'amazed', 'delighted', 'miserable', 'gorgeous', 'extraordinary', etc. 'Terrible' means 'extremely bad', so we cannot make it any stronger by putting 'very' in front of it. However, we can put 'really' or 'absolutely' in front of these adjectives.

1 **The food was really terrible.**
その料理は、とてもまずかった。

2 **The weather was ∧ wonderful.**
天気はすばらしかった。

3 **They live in an ∧ enormous house.**
彼らはものすごく大きな家に住んでいます。

Common Mistake 85

✕ The party was very fun.

very funと言うことはできませんが、good fun、great fun、a lot of fun、really funと言うことはできます。
We cannot say 'very fun'. Instead, we say 'good fun', 'great fun', 'a lot of fun' or 'really fun'.

〇 **The party was good fun.**
The party was a lot of fun.
パーティはとても楽しかった。

Common Mistake 86

✕1 I was angry very much.

✕2 It was raining heavily very much.

形容詞や副詞のあとにvery muchをつけることはできません。形容詞や副詞の前でveryを使います。
We do not use 'very much' after an adjective or adverb. We use 'very' before adjectives and adverbs.

① **I was very angry.**
私はとても腹を立てました。

② **It was raining very heavily.**
とてもひどい雨でした。

Common Mistake 87

 I have never met a so kind person.

《形容詞＋名詞》の前ではsuch (a) を使います。形容詞だけの場合はsoを使います。

'Such (a)' is used before adjectives which are followed by a noun. 'So' is used before adjectives which are not followed by a noun.

 **I have never met such a kind person.**

そんなに優しい人に会ったことがありません。

- She's so stupid.

  彼女は本当に馬鹿です。

《so＋形容詞＋a＋名詞》という形（例えばso kind a man）もありますが、文語的で古く、あまり使われない表現です。

There is a structure 'so' + adjective + 'a' + noun (e.g. 'so kind a man') but it is rather literary and old-fashioned, and is not commonly used.

Common Mistake 88

 I have ever been to America.

「〜したことがある」というような肯定文の中にeverは使えません。
'Ever' is not used in sentences of this type. We should say:

 **I have ^ been to America.**

私はアメリカへ行ったことがあります。

everは主に、疑問文中、ifのあと、形容詞の最上級のあとの節で使われます。
'Ever' is mostly used in questions, after 'if' and after superlative adjectives (e.g. 'the biggest', 'the best').

- Have you **ever** been to America?
  (これまでに) アメリカへ行ったことがありますか。
- If you **ever** come to Kyoto, please come and see me.
  もし (いつか) 京都へいらっしゃることがありましたら、どうぞ私のところにいらしてください。
- He's the strangest person I've **ever** met.
  彼は私が今までに会った人の中で一番変わった人です。

Common Mistake 89

✗1 Recently Korean movies are very popular.

✗2 Recently many women have jobs.

recentlyは「今から少し前」という意味なので、現在時制の動詞と一緒に使うことはできません。現在の状況を話しているのならnowadaysやthese daysを使います。

'Recently' means 'a short time ago', so it cannot be used with a verb in the present tense. If we are talking about a present situation, we say 'nowadays' or 'these days'.

1 **Korean movies are very popular nowadays.**
最近、韓国の映画が大はやりです。

2 **Many women have jobs these days.**
このごろは、多くの女性が仕事を持っています。

recentlyは、それほど遠くない過去に始まって、今もなお続いていることについて話すときに、現在完了と一緒に使います。

We use 'recently' with the present perfect tense (i.e. 'has become') when we are talking about a situation which started not long ago and is still continuing now.

- Korean movies have become very popular recently.
  最近、韓国の映画がとてもはやってきています。
- The weather has been strange recently.
  このごろの天気はおかしい。

また、近い過去に起こってもう終わったことには、過去時制と一緒にrecentlyを使います。

When we are talking about a completed action which happened in the recent past, we use 'recently' with the simple past tense.

- I heard a funny story recently.
  最近笑い話を聞きました。
- I saw a very good movie recently.
  最近とてもいい映画を見ました。

Common Mistake 90

✗1 After all, we got home at 2 a.m.

✗2 We waited for forty minutes and then, after all, the bus arrived.

after allは「最後に」という意味の「結局」ではありません。「最後に」の意味を表すにはfinally、または長い間待ったり遅れたりしたあとに何かが起きたのなら、at lastを使います。

'After all' does not mean 'at the end'. We should say 'finally' instead, or if something happened after a long wait or delay, we say 'at last'.

1 **We finally got home at 2 a.m.**
私たちは午前2時にやっと家に着きました。

2 **We waited for forty minutes and then, at last, the bus arrived.**
私たちは40分待ちました。そしてついにバスがやって来ました。

after allは、作文や文書の結論を持ち出すときに使うものではありません。そのような場合は、in conclusionを使います。

'After all' should not be used to introduce the conclusion of a composition or piece of writing. Instead, one should say 'in conclusion'.

● **In conclusion**, I think Japan should not build any more nuclear power stations.
結論として、日本はこれ以上原子力発電所を建設すべきではないと思います。

after all が節の終わりにあるときは、「予想に反して（結局）～」や「前にこう言ったけれど結局～」という意味です。
When 'after all' is at the end of a clause, it means 'contrary to expectations' or 'in spite of what was said before'.

● I thought I was going to be late, but I was on time **after all**.
遅れると思いましたが、結局、間に合いました。

● I'm sorry, I can't help you **after all**.
〈お手伝いできると思ったのに〉結局お手伝いできなくて、ごめんなさい。

節の初めにafter all があるときは、たった今言ったことの重要な理由がそのあとに続きます。
When 'after all' is at the beginning of a clause, it introduces an important reason for something which has just been said.

● Let's go and see Jeff. **After all**, it may be our last chance to see him before he goes to China.
ジェフに会いに行きましょう。これが、彼が中国に行く前に彼に会える最後のチャンスになるかもしれませんから。

Exercise 4

次の文中の間違いを見つけて正しい英語に直してください。それぞれの文末のかっこ内の数は、間違いの数を示しています。答えは巻末にあります。

1. I was exciting very much when I heard the news. (2)

____

2. I always feel ashamed when I have to give a speech. (1)

____

3. America is very wide. (1)

____

4. In London parks are many. (1)

____

5. At this university foreign students are many. (1)

____

6. My wages are very cheap. (1)

____

7. I think Mr. Takada is very pretty. (1)

____

8. I want to save much money and buy car. (2)

____

9. I was very painful. (1)

____

10. In Japan, most of people is tired most of the time. (2)

____

11. Almost of young Japanese girl is shy. (3)

✎ ____________________

12. The weather was very terrible, but we enjoyed very much. (2)

✎ ____________________

13. The trip was very fun. (1)

✎ ____________________

14. We talked until 3 a.m. and then, after all, we went home. (1)

✎ ____________________

15. I have ever been to New Zealand. (1)

✎ ____________________

16. I was very enjoyable. (1)

✎ ____________________

17. Recently many Japanese people read comics. (1)

✎ ____________________

18. Swimming in sea on hot, sunny day is very interesting. (3)

✎ ____________________

19. I am very hard to learn German grammar. (1)

✎ ____________________

20. I thought I was going to die, so I was really terrible. (1)

✎ ____________________

21. I like horror movies because they are terrible. (1)

✎ ____________________

22. He is half. (1)

✎ ______________________________

23. Every Japanese schoolchildren have to learn English. (1)

✎ ______________________________

24. There are too many students in this college, so I feel it is narrow. (1)

✎ ______________________________

25. In Japan English people is few. (2)

✎ ______________________________

26. I couldn't understand the teacher, so I was boring. (1)

✎ ______________________________

27. At high school I was absorbed in music. (1)

✎ ______________________________

28. During the World War II, food was little in Japan. (2)

✎ ______________________________

Chapter 5

名詞に関する間違い

Problems with Nouns

Common Mistake 91

✕ 1 My hometown is very country.

My hometown is countryside.

✕ 2 Akita Prefecture is very country.

💡 第一に、countryやcountrysideは日本語の「田舎」とまったく同じ意味ではありません。countryやcountrysideは、建物がほとんどない畑や野山ばかりのところを意味するので、「町is country」とか「町is countryside」と言うことはできません。また、決してvery countryとは言いません。英語では「町や村is in the country」とか「田舎の地域is rural」という言い方をします。

第二に、hometownという言葉は常に「町」、すなわち人家や建物がたくさん建ち並んでいるところという意味合いを持っているので、小さな村や畑、野山の中に家がある場合は、その場所をhometownと呼ぶことはできません。

Firstly, 'country' and 'countryside' do not mean exactly the same as the Japanese word *inaka*. 'Country' and 'countryside' mean 'land which is not covered with buildings', so we cannot say that a town is 'country' or 'countryside'. Also, we never say 'very country'. Instead, we say that a town or village is 'in the country', and we say that a country district is 'rural'.
Secondly, the word 'hometown' always refers to a town, i.e. a large group of buildings, so if one's home is in a small village or in the middle of fields and mountains, one should not call that place one's 'hometown'.

1 **My hometown is in the country [countryside].**

私の故郷は田舎町です。

I come from the country [countryside].

私は田舎から出て来ました→私の故郷は田舎です。

I come from a small town [village] in the country [countryside].

私の故郷は田舎の小さい町［村］です。

② **Akita Prefecture is very rural.**

秋田県はとても田舎です。

Common Mistake 92

× I went back to my country in Gifu Prefecture.

countryには「故郷」という意味はないので、my countryと言ったら「私の国」、すなわち日本やアメリカ、英国などという意味になってしまいます。故郷という意味の「国」はhometownやhomeです。

'Country' does not mean 'hometown'. 'My country' means 'my nation', i.e. Japan, America, Britain, etc.

I went back to my hometown in Gifu Prefecture.

私は岐阜県にある故郷へ帰りました。

Common Mistake **93**

 My hometown is ∧ Hyogo Prefecture.

 My hometown is Sadо Island.

hometownは生まれ育った町、または子ども時代を過ごした町という意味なので、県や地方や島などの、町でない場所を指すことはできません。

'Hometown' means 'the town where one was born and/or brought up', so it cannot refer to any place other than a town.

 **My hometown is in Hyogo Prefecture.**

私の故郷は兵庫県です。

● My **hometown** is Himeji in Hyogo Prefecture.

私の**故郷**は兵庫県姫路市です。

② **I come from Sado Island.**

私は佐渡ヶ島出身です。

Common Mistake 94

✗1 Ginza is a very expensive town.

✗2 Umeda is a very busy town.

townは自治体とふつうはその長（市長、町長など）を持つ、家やビルが集まった広い地域のことです。cityより小さく、villageより大きいところです。**例えば鎌倉、日光、軽井沢、宇治、宝塚などです（cityは東京、大阪、名古屋などです）。**cityの一部分はtownではなくareaやdistrictです。**銀座や梅田は東京、大阪の一部なのでareaあるいはdistrictです。**

A town is a large group of houses and other buildings with its own municipal government, and usually a mayor. It is smaller than a city and larger than a village. Here are some examples of Japanese towns: Kamakura, Nikko, Karuizawa, Uji, Takarazuka.
If we are talking about a part of a city, we say 'area' or 'district'. Ginza is part of Tokyo, and Umeda is part of Osaka City, so they are 'areas' or 'districts', not 'towns'.

1 Ginza is a very expensive area.

銀座は物価の高いところです。

2 Umeda is a very busy district.

梅田はにぎやかなところです。

Common Mistake 95

✗1 Japanese work very hard.

✗2 His wife is a Japanese.

「日本人」(複数) はふつう、Japanese people または the Japanese と言います。the Japanese の方が Japanese people よりも形式的です。

The people of Japan are usually called 'Japanese people' or 'the Japanese'. 'The Japanese' is more formal than 'Japanese people'.

① **The Japanese work very hard.**

Japanese people work very hard.

日本人はよく働きます。

ただし、many Japanese, most Japanese と言うことはできます。

However, we can say 'many Japanese' and 'most Japanese'.

- Many Japanese live and work abroad nowadays.
  このごろはたくさんの日本人が海外に住み、働いています。

「(1人の) 日本人」は a Japanese man/woman/person、または形容詞の Japanese を使います。

When talking about a single Japanese person, we say 'a Japanese man/woman/person', or we use the adjective 'Japanese'.

② **His wife is Japanese.**

彼の奥さんは日本人です。

He married a Japanese woman.

彼は日本人女性と結婚しました。

辞書や文法の本によれば、a Japaneseと言うことは可能ですが、ネイティブスピーカーはめったにa Japaneseとは言いません。
According to dictionaries and grammar books it is possible to say 'a Japanese', but native speakers of English hardly ever say this.

Common Mistake **96**

✕1 I met some very interesting persons at the party.

✕2 I was interviewed by two persons.

personの複数形personsは、主に非常に改まった場合に使います。形式にこだわらない日常の英語ではpeopleと言います。
The word 'persons' is mainly used in very formal English. In normal everyday English we say 'people' rather than 'persons'.

1 **I met some very interesting people at the party.**
パーティでおもしろい人たちに会いました。

2 **I was interviewed by two people.**
私は（面接官が）2人の面接を受けました。

personは、ふつう単数形として使われます。
'Person' is usually used in the singular.

● He's a nice person.
彼はすてきな人です。

Common Mistake 97

✕1 I have lots of boyfriends but I don't have a sweetheart.

✕2 I met my lover in junior high school.

第一に、boyfriendやgirlfriendは、ふつう「恋人」を意味します（ただし、女性が同性の友達をgirlfriendと言うことはあります）。ただの異性の友達はmale friendやfemale friend、woman friend（複数形はwomen friends）と言います。

第二に、sweetheartという英語は時代遅れで、今はめったに使われません。

第三に、loverはふつう婚外の恋愛関係の相手を意味します。独身者はmy loverとは言いません。

Firstly, 'boyfriend' and 'girlfriend' usually mean 'a person with whom one is having a romantic and/or sexual relationship'. (However, women sometimes use the word 'girlfriend' meaning 'female friend'.) When talking about friends of the opposite sex with whom we do not have a romantic relationship, we say 'male friends' or 'female friends' or 'women friends'.
Secondly, the word 'sweetheart' is old-fashioned, and is seldom used.
Thirdly, a person's 'lover' usually means a partner in an extramarital relationship. Single people do not use the expression 'my lover'.

1 I have lots of male friends but I don't have a boyfriend.

私には男友達はたくさんいますが、恋人はいません。

2 I met my girlfriend in junior high school.

僕は中学校でガールフレンドと知り合いました。

● She went to Australia with a **girlfriend**.

彼女は女友達とオーストラリアへ行きました。

Common Mistake 98

✕1 the master of the shop

✕2 the master of the restaurant

店やレストラン、バーの経営者や支配人は、masterではなくmanagerで、持ち主はownerです。イギリス英語では、店やレストラン、バーの女性の経営者や支配人をmanageressと言います。

The person who manages a shop, restaurant or bar is called the 'manager', not the 'master'. The person who owns it is called the 'owner'. In British English, a woman who manages a shop, restaurant or bar is called the 'manageress'.

1 **the manager of the shop**

この店の店長

2 **the manager of the restaurant**

レストランの支配人

現代の英語でmasterという名詞の一番よく使われる意味は、次の通りです。

The most common uses of the noun 'master' in modern English are as follows:

1. 調教された動物、特に犬の飼い主
   the master of a trained animal, especially a dog
2. 工芸、手工芸等特殊技術の名人や優れた芸術家
   a master craftsman or artist
3. 修士（号）
   a Master's (degree)

5 名詞に関する間違い

Common Mistake 99

✗1 French dishes are more delicious than English dishes.

✗2 I miss my mother's dishes.

「料理」はfoodあるいはcookingです。特定の国や地方、レストランの料理にはfoodを使い、特定の人が作った料理にはcookingを使います。

The Japanese word *ryori* should be translated as 'food' or 'cooking'. We use 'food' to talk about the food of a particular country, region or restaurant, and 'cooking' to talk about the food cooked by a particular person.

1 **French food is more delicious than English food.**

フランス料理はイギリス料理よりおいしい。

2 **I miss my mother's cooking.**

母の料理が恋しい。

dishの基本的な意味は、料理を盛る大皿のことで、この皿から料理が銘々に取り分けられます。複数形のdishesは食事のときに使う食器類やナイフ、フォーク類のすべてのことです。

The basic meaning of 'dish' is 'a container for serving food at meals'. The plural 'dishes' means 'all the crockery and cutlery used at a meal'.

- Have you got a dish to put the vegetables in?
  野菜を入れるお皿はありますか。
- I'll wash the dishes.
  私が皿洗いをします。

dishのもう1つの意味は「皿に盛られた料理」、あるいは「料理の種類」のことです。

Another meaning of 'dish' is 'some cooked food on a dish', or 'a type of cooked food'.

- In a Chinese restaurant it's best to order lots of **dishes** and then share them.
  中国料理店では、いろいろな料理を注文して分け合うのが一番いい。
- Yorkshire Pudding is an English **dish** eaten with roast beef.
  ヨークシャープディングはローストビーフと一緒に食べるイギリス料理です。

Common Mistake 100

✕ The doctor gave me an injection in my hip.

「お尻」はbottomまたは形式的でないアメリカ英語でbuttです。hipというのは、脚よりも上でウエストより下の、体の左右に張り出した部分の一方のことで、両方を指すときはhipsと言います。

The part of the body on which one sits is called the 'bottom', or 'butt' in informal American English. 'Hip' means the side of the body above the legs and below the waist.

The doctor gave me an injection in my bottom.

医者が私のお尻に注射をしました。

Common Mistake 101

✕1 My favorite sport is ski.

✕2 Ski is exciting.

スポーツ名の「スキー」はskiingです。
The sport in which one goes down mountains on skis is called 'skiing'.

1. **My favorite sport is skiing.**
   私の好きなスポーツはスキーです。
2. **Skiing is exciting.**
   スキーはわくわくします。

名詞skiは、「スキーの板」という意味です。
The noun 'ski' means the thing attached to the foot used in skiing.

- I bought a pair of skis.
  私はスキー〈の板を1組〉を買いました。

skiは動詞にもなります。
'Ski' is also a verb.

- I've never skied in Japan.
  日本でスキーをしたことはありません。

Common Mistake 102

Did you have a good travel?

名詞travelの意味は「(一般的な意味の) 旅行」です。1つの特定の旅行を指す場合は、journeyやtripを使います。

The noun 'travel' means 'traveling in general'. When we are talking about a particular piece of travel, we say 'journey' or 'trip'.

Did you have a good trip?

Did you have a good journey?

いい旅でしたか。

- My hobbies are music and travel.
  私の趣味は音楽と旅行です。

journeyとtripの違いは、journeyがある場所から別の場所への移動のみを表すのに対し、tripは目的地までの移動と、そこでしたこと、さらに帰って来ることのすべてを表しています。

The difference between 'journey' and 'trip' is that 'journey' refers only to the movement from one place to another, whereas a 'trip' means both the journey to a place and what one does at one's destination, and also the return journey.

Common Mistake 103

~~1~~ In the summer many people leave dust on the beach.

~~2~~ In my town we have to divide dust into two categories.

現代英語でdustの意味は「ほこり」です。「ごみ」は、アメリカ英語ではtrashまたはgarbage、イギリス英語ではrubbishと言います。紙くずや空き缶などの地面に落ちているごみはlitterとも言います。

In modern English 'dust' means *hokori*. *Gomi* is called 'trash' or 'garbage' in America, and 'rubbish' in Britain. Pieces of trash lying on the ground, such as paper, cans, etc., can also be called 'litter'.

1 **In the summer many people leave trash on the beach.**

夏にはたくさんの人が海岸にごみを捨てていきます。

2 **In my town we have to divide garbage into two categories.**

私の町では、ごみは２種類に分別しなければなりません。

- The top of the piano was covered with dust.

そのピアノはほこりをかぶっていました。

Common Mistake 104

 I threw it into the dust box.

「ごみ箱」は、アメリカ英語ではtrash canまたはgarbage canと言います。イギリス英語ではいくつかの言い方があります。キッチンのごみ箱はrubbish bin、ふつうの部屋やオフィスなどではwastepaper basket、公園や道路、公共の場所ではlitter binまたはrubbish binと言います。家庭の屋外に置いてある大きなごみ容器はdustbinです。

A receptacle for trash is called a 'trash can' or 'garbage can' in American English. In British English, there are several different words. In a kitchen it is called a 'rubbish bin'. In an office or a room other than a kitchen, it is called a 'wastepaper basket'. In a park, street or public place, it is called a 'litter bin' or 'rubbish bin'. A large container for rubbish outside a house is called a 'dustbin'.

 **I threw it into the trash can.** (アメリカ英語)

I threw it in the rubbish bin. (イギリス英語)

私はそれをごみ箱に捨てました。

Common Mistake **105**

✗1 My hobby is watching television.

✗2 My hobby is shopping.

hobbyというのは、楽しむために行う、ある程度の技術を必要とする活動のことで、例えば、写真撮影、絵画、ピアノ演奏、ガーデニングなどです。やればやるほどその技術が上達するような活動です。テレビを見たり買い物をすることは、それほど技能を必要としないので、hobbyとは言いません。

A hobby is an activity that one does for pleasure and which requires some skill, for example, photography, painting, playing the piano, gardening, etc. The more one does these activities, the more one develops one's skill at them. We cannot call watching television and shopping 'hobbies' as they do not require much skill.

1 I love **watching television.**

テレビを見るのが大好きです → 私の趣味はテレビを見ることです。

2 I really enjoy **shopping.**

私は買い物が本当に好きです → 私の趣味はショッピングです。

Common Mistake **106**

✗1 Most juice contains a lot of sugar, so I try not to drink it.

✗2 All over Japan there are vending machines selling juice, beer and cigarettes.

英語のjuiceの意味は、日本語の「ジュース」と同じではありません。juiceは果物や野菜に含まれる水分、またはそれをしぼったもののことです。日本でジュースと言われている砂糖や香料を加えたアルコールの入っていない飲み物は、juiceではなくsoft drinkと言います。

The meaning of the English word 'juice' is not the same as the Japanese word *juusu*. 'Juice' means the liquid in fruit and vegetables, or the liquid which is squeezed out of fruit or vegetables. A non-alcoholic drink containing sugar, flavoring, etc., is called a 'soft drink', not 'juice'.

1. **Most soft drinks contain a lot of sugar, so I try not to drink them.**

   たいていのジュース［ソフトドリンク］は砂糖がたくさん入っているので、飲まないようにしています。

2. **All over Japan there are vending machines selling soft drinks, beer and cigarettes.**

   日本にはジュース［ソフトドリンク］とビールとたばこの自動販売機がたくさんあります。

オレンジ果汁が100%未満の飲み物は、orange juiceではなく、orange drinkと言います。

A drink containing less than 100% orange juice is called 'orange drink', not 'orange juice'.

Common Mistake 107

✕ At my high school we were not allowed to wear pierce.

「耳飾り」は英語ではすべてearringです。耳は2つあるので、ふつうは複数形で使われます。耳に穴をあけてつける耳飾りのことを、日本語では「ピアス」と言いますが、英語のpierceは「刺す」とか「小さな穴をあける」という意味の動詞です。

An ornament worn on the ear is called an ‘earring’. Since we have two ears, this word is often plural. ‘Pierce’ is a verb meaning to make a hole with a sharp instrument.

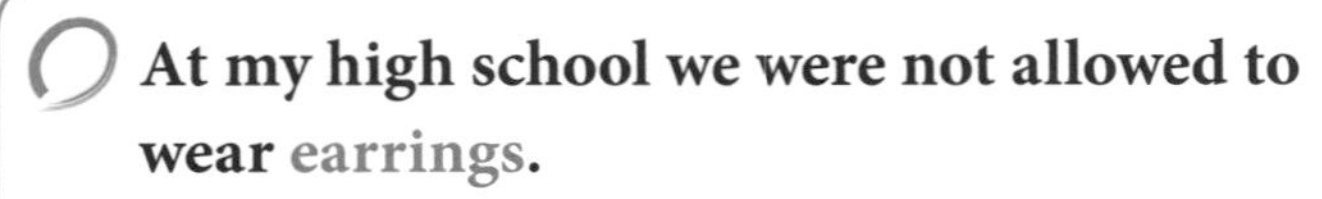

At my high school we were not allowed to wear earrings.

私の高校では、イヤリングは禁止されていました。

● I had my ears **pierced**.

私は耳に穴を開けました。

Common Mistake 108

✗1 Who is Prime Minister of England?

✗2 The English government usually supports the US.

日本語で「英国」または「イギリス」と呼ばれている国は、英語ではBritain, the United Kingdomあるいはthe UKと言います。England（イングランド）はこの国の一地域で、ほかにScotland（スコットランド）、Wales（ウェールズ）、Northern Ireland（北アイルランド）と呼ばれる地域があります。

The country which is called *Eikoku* or *Igirisu* in Japanese is called 'Britain' or 'the United Kingdom' or 'the UK' in English. England is one part of this country, together with Scotland, Wales and Northern Ireland.

1 Who is Prime Minister of Britain?

イギリスの総理大臣はだれですか。

2 The British government usually supports the US.

イギリスの政府はたいていアメリカを支持します。

厳密に言えば、Britainとthe United Kingdomは違います。BritainはEngland, Scotland, Walesの3つの地方のことで、the United Kingdomはその3つとさらにNorthern Irelandも含みます。とはいえ、Britainという語は通例はthe United Kingdomと同じ意味で使われます。

Strictly speaking, there is a difference between 'Britain' and 'the United Kingdom'. 'Britain' means England, Scotland and Wales, whereas 'the United Kingdom' means England, Scotland, Wales and Northern Ireland. However, the word 'Britain' is commonly used with the same meaning as 'the United Kingdom'.

Common Mistake 109

 She sent me a mail saying she was sick.

「電子メール」の意味で使われる日本語の「メール」は、mailではなく、emailまたはtextです。

The Japanese word *meeru* should be translated as 'email' or 'text', not 'mail'.

She sent me an email saying she was sick.
彼女から病気だというメールが来ました。

mailの意味は、アメリカ英語では、郵便局が配達する手紙や小包などのことです。（イギリス英語ではpostです）。mailは数えられない名詞です。

In American English, 'mail' means letters, packages, etc., which are delivered by the post office. (In British English we say 'post'.) 'Mail' is an uncountable noun.

- What time does the mail usually come?
  郵便はいつも何時ごろ来ますか。

Common Mistake 110

The teacher gives us a print at the beginning of every lesson.

教師が生徒に配る印刷物や、講演などでの配布資料はprintではなく、handoutと言います。

A piece of printed paper which a teacher gives students, or which is handed out to people listening to a lecture or talk, is called a 'handout', not a 'print'.

The teacher gives us a handout at the beginning of every lesson.

毎回授業の初めに、先生はプリントを私たちに配ります。

Common Mistake 111

× My father is a salaryman.

My father is a salaried man.

「サラリーマン」という言葉は和製英語です。ネイティブスピーカーは次のような表現をします。

The word 'salaryman' is a Japanese invention. A native speaker would say:

My father works in an office.

父はサラリーマンです。

しかし、salarymanという言葉は、日本に関する英文記事や本の中でよく使われ、その意味は「日本人のサラリーマン」です。また日本に住む外国人はよくsalarymanを使います。たとえば、次のようにです。

However, the word 'salaryman' is often used in English-language articles and books about Japan, meaning a male Japanese office worker. Also, foreigners who live in Japan often use the word 'salaryman'. For example,

- Thanks to the pandemic, Japanese **salarymen** can get more sleep.
  パンデミック（流行病）のおかげで、日本のサラリーマンはより長い時間眠ることができる。
- My girlfriend's father is a typical **salaryman**.
  僕のガールフレンドのお父さんは、典型的なサラリーマンです。

和英辞書では、「サラリーマン」はsalaried manやsalaried workerとなっていますが、ネイティブスピーカーはめったにこれらの表現を使いません。

In Japanese-English dictionaries *sarariiman* is translated as 'salaried man' or 'salaried worker', but these expressions are rarely used by native speakers.

Common Mistake 112

✕1 I am a safety driver.

✕2 I will be safety driver from now on.

safetyは名詞なので、safety driverと言うことはできません。次のように言います。

'Safety' is a noun, so one cannot say 'safety driver'. One should say:

① **I am a safe driver.**

私は安全運転のドライバーです。

② **I will drive safely from now on.**

私はこれから安全運転をします。

Common Mistake 113

✕1 I live in a small mansion.

✕2 They pulled down the old house and built a mansion.

mansionの意味は、とても裕福な人が所有していて部屋数が少なくとも20くらいはある、非常に大きな家のことです。日本語のマンションの1世帯分を、アメリカ英語ではapartment、イギリス英語ではflatと言います。マンションの建物全体をアメリカ英語ではapartment building、イギリス英語ではblock of flatsと言います。

'Mansion' means an extremely large house with at least 20 rooms, belonging to a very wealthy person. A Japanese *manshon*, meaning the place where one household lives, is called an 'apartment' in American English, or a 'flat' in British English. A building which contains many apartments is called an 'apartment building' in American English, or a 'block of flats' in British English.

1 **I live in a small apartment.**

私は小さなマンションに住んでいます。〈アメリカ英語〉

I live in a small flat.

私は小さなマンションに住んでいます。〈イギリス英語〉

2 **They pulled down the old house and built an apartment building.**

彼らは古い家を取り壊して、マンションを建てました。

分譲マンションのことを、アメリカ英語でcondominiumあるいはcondoとも言います。

An apartment which can be bought and sold can also be called a 'condominium' or 'condo' in American English.

● Curtis bought a **condominium** in Hawaii.
カーティスはハワイにマンション［コンドミニアム］を買いました。

イギリスでは、mansionの複数形mansionsは、マンション（の建物全体）の名前として使われることがあります。例えば、Kensington Mansionsというようにです。これが日本語の「マンション」のもとなのかもしれません。
In Britain, the plural word 'Mansions' is sometimes used in the name of a block of flats, for example 'Kensington Mansions'. This may be the origin of the Japanese word *manshon*.

Common Mistake 114

✕ 1 Foxes sleep during the day and hunt at midnight.

✕ 2 I like looking at the stars at midnight.

at midnightは「夜の12時に」という意味です。「夜中に」とか「真夜中に」と言いたいときは、at nightやin the middle of the nightを使います。
'At midnight' means 'at 12 p.m.'. If we do not mean the exact time, we should say 'at night' or 'in the middle of the night'.

① **Foxes sleep during the day and hunt at night.**
キツネは昼間は眠り、夜、獲物をとります。

② **I like looking at the stars at night.**
私は夜、星をながめるのが好きです。

Common Mistake 115

✕1 I was in trouble in France because I can't speak French.

✕2 The fees of this university are very high, so my parents are in trouble.

be in troubleはふつう悪いことをして警察に捕まったり、上司や先生などの権力者に見つかるという意味です。あるいは、とても危険な状況にある場合にも使います。

それ以外で、何も悪いことをしていないし危険にもさらされていないけれど、困難な状況にあるときは、have a hard timeやbe in difficultyを使います。

When we say that someone is 'in trouble', we usually mean that they have done something bad and have been caught by the police, or by an authority such as their boss or teacher. Alternatively, we can say that someone is 'in trouble' if they are in a very dangerous situation.
In other situations, we say that someone 'has a hard time' or 'is in difficulty' when we mean that they are in a difficult situation, but have not done anything bad, and are not in danger.

1 **I had a hard time in France because I can't speak French.**
フランス語が話せないので、フランスでは困りました。

2 **The fees of this university are very high, so my parents are having a hard time.**
この大学の学費はとても高いので、私の両親は苦労しています。

● He's in trouble with the police because he was caught driving without a license.
彼は無免許運転で警察につかまって厄介なことになっています。

Exercise 5

次の文中の間違いを見つけて正しい英語に直してください。それぞれの文末のかっこ内の数は、間違いの数を示しています。答えは巻末にあります。

1. My hometown is Hokkaido. (1)

______

2. My hometown is very country. (1)

______

3. Many Japanese people go back to their country at the New Year. (1)

______

4. I hate being woken by the telephone at midnight. (1)

______

5. I had a pleasant travel. (1)

______

6. Before the war Japanese were poorer than now. (1)

______

7. When I was in America I was in trouble to eat American food. (1)

______

8. There were a lot of persons in the park. (1)

______

9. My hobby is music, swimming and ski. (3)

______

10. Harajuku is very fashionable town in Tokyo. (2)

____

11. My mother's dishes are delicious. (1)

____

12. He is a salaryman. (1)

____

13. The master of the restaurant is very kind. (1)

____

14. My hobby is shopping. (1)

____

15. The teacher uses prints instead of a textbook. (1)

____

16. Japanese people throw away a lot of dust every day. (1)

____

17. Please put your dust in the dust box. (2)

____

18. Most juice contains a lot of sugar and artificial chemicals. (1)

____

19. Many Japanese people live in mansions. (1)

____

20. He wears pierce. (1)

____

21. I want to be a safety driver. (1)

____

22. England has much higher taxes than Japan. (1)

____

23. I like sending mails to my friends. (1)

____

Chapter 6

前置詞・接続詞に関する間違い

Problems with Prepositions and Conjunctions

Common Mistake **116**

✕1 I spent five days at Kyushu.

✕2 My parents live at Nagano Prefecture.

✕3 We played mahjong at my room.

広い場所やまわりに境界線のある場所、例えば、国、地方、町、大きな島、公園、庭などとともに使う前置詞は、atではなくinです。
We use 'in' with any large area, or any area with a boundary around it, such as a country, region, town, large island, park, garden, etc.

1 **I spent five days in Kyushu.**
私は九州で5日過ごしました。

2 **My parents live in Nagano Prefecture.**
私の両親は長野県に住んでいます。

部屋、箱、バッグなど立体的なもの「の中で［に］」と言うときも、inを使います。
We also use 'in' when we mean 'inside a three-dimensional space', such as a room, box, bag, etc.

3 **We played mahjong in my room.**
私たちは私の部屋でマージャンをしました。

実際の大きさがない地点について「〜で」と言うときは、atを使います。
We use 'at' with points which do not have any real size.

- I live at the end of the street.
私は通りの突き当たりに住んでいます。

● Turn right **at** the second traffic lights.
2つ目の信号で右に曲がってください。

出来事が起こるのが建物の中か外ではなく、何が起こるかに主な関心がある場合も、場所（ふつう建物）の名前とともにatを使います。

We also use 'at' with the name of a place (usually a building) when we are mainly interested in what happens there, and not in whether the action takes place inside or outside the building.

● I'll meet you **at** the station.
駅でお目にかかりましょう。

● We met **at** the club.
私たちはクラブで会いました。

● She teaches **at** a high school.
彼女は高校で教えています。

上の例では、駅、クラブ、学校で起こることに関心があります。建物の中か外かは重要ではありません。

In these sentences we are interested in what happens at the station, club or school. It does not matter whether the action is physically inside or outside the station, club or school.

Common Mistake 117

✗1 I'm going to Shinshu on next Saturday.

✗2 I was very busy in last month.

✗3 What did you do at the summer?

✗4 What are you going to do on Chistmas?

時を表す名詞の前にthis, next, last, that, everyがあるときは、その前にin, at, onはつけません。

We do not use 'in', 'at', 'on' before 'this', 'next', 'last', 'that' or 'every' when they are used before a time expression.

① **I'm going to Shinshu ∧ next Saturday.**
来週の土曜日、信州へ出かけます。

② **I was very busy ∧ last month.**
先月はとても忙しかったです。

1日より長い時間、例えば月、季節、年、世紀、時代などの前にはinを使います。

We use 'in' with any period of time longer than a day, i.e. a month, season, year, century, historical period, etc.

③ **What did you do in the summer?**
夏に何をしましたか。

● I was born in 1956.
私は1956年に生まれました。

時間上の1点を表すときは、atを使います。例えばat 9 o'clock, at midnightなどです。また、「何かの始めに」at the beginning of ～ とか、「何かの終わりに」at the end of ～ というときもatを使います。

We use 'at' with points in time, for example, 'at 9 o'clock', 'at midnight'. We also say 'at the beginning of (something)' and 'at the end of (something)'.

次のような（数日間続く）休日の前にもatを使います。at Christmas, at (the) New Year, at Easter, at Thanksgivingなどです。しかし、そのうちの1日のみを指す場合はonを使います。on Christmas Day, on New Year's Dayなどです。

We also say 'at' before certain holiday periods: 'at Christmas', 'at (the) New Year', 'at Easter' and 'at Thanksgiving'. However, we say 'on' when we talk about one day of the holiday, i.e. 'on Christmas Day', 'on New Year's Day'.

What are you going to do at Chistmas?

クリスマスに何をしますか。

● What are you going to do on Christmas Day?

クリスマスの日に何をしますか。

Common Mistake 118

✗1 I see my parents about twice in a month.

✗2 I work as a waitress three times in a week.

動作の頻度を言うときは、inは使いません。
We do not use 'in' when talking about the frequency of an action.

① **I see my parents about twice ∧ a month.**
私は両親に1カ月に2回くらい会います。

② **I work as a waitress three times ∧ a week.**
私は1週間に3回ウェイトレスとして働きます。

Common Mistake 119

~~1~~ I'll call you again after three days.

~~2~~ I look forward to seeing you after two weeks.

~~3~~ I'm going to America three weeks later.

未来のことを話すときはin three daysまたはin three days' timeと言います。過去のことなら、three days laterまたはafter three daysと言います。
When we are talking about the future, we say 'in three days' or 'in three days' time'. When we are talking about the past, we say 'three days later' or 'after three days'.

1. **I'll call you again in three days.**
   3日後にまたお電話します。
2. **I look forward to seeing you in two weeks.**
   2週間後にお目にかかれるのを楽しみにしています。
3. **I'm going to America in three weeks' time.**
   3週間後アメリカへ発ちます。

- Three days later he died.
  After three days he died.
  3日後に彼は死にました。

Common Mistake 120

✗1 My parents told me to come home until 10 o'clock.

✗2 I have to finish reading this book till Friday.

「～までに（は）」、「～より遅くなく」という意味（完了の期限）を表すときは、byを使います。「～まで（ずっと）」という意味（継続の終了時点）を表すときは、until, tillを使います。

'By' before a point in time means 'not later than'. 'Until' and 'till' are used to say when an action or state finishes.

1 **My parents told me to come home by 10 o'clock.**

両親は10時までに帰宅するようにと言いました。

2 **I have to finish reading this book by Friday.**

この本を金曜日までに読み終えなければなりません。

- I slept until 11 o'clock.

  私は11時まで眠りました。

- We waited till midnight.

  夜の12時まで私たちは持ちました。

Common Mistake 121

✕1 He wrote a book during he was in prison.

✕2 We can chat during we are working.

動詞を含む節の前では、duringではなくwhileを使います。
'While', not 'during', is used before a clause containing a verb.

1 **He wrote a book while he was in prison.**
彼は刑務所にいる間に本を書きました。

2 **We can chat while we are working.**
私たちは仕事をしながらおしゃべりができます。

duringは期間を表す名詞の前に使います。
'During' is used before nouns which refer to periods of time.

- during the summer
  夏の間
- during the night
  夜の間
- during the war
  戦争中

Common Mistake 122

✗1 He walked away with smiling to himself.

✗2 I like listening to music with driving.

✗3 I usually read the newspaper with eating breakfast.

「〜しながら」という意味の現在分詞を使った文で、主節の主語と現在分詞の主語が同じであるときは、現在分詞節の前にwithは使いません。

'With' is not used before a present participle clause if the subject of that clause is the same as the subject of the main clause. We should say:

1 **He walked away ∧ smiling to himself.**

彼は笑いながら通り過ぎて行きました。

同じ主語によって、2つの長い動作が同時に行われることを強調したいときは、現在分詞の前にwhileを使います。

If we want to emphasize that two long actions by the same subject happen at the same time, we use 'while' before a present participle.

2 **I like listening to music while driving.**

ドライブ中、音楽を聞くのが好きです。

3 **I usually read the newspaper while eating breakfast.**

私はたいてい朝食を食べながら新聞を読みます。

また、主節の主語と現在分詞の主語が異なるときは、現在分詞節の前にwithを使います。
We use 'with' before a present participle clause if the subject of that clause is different from the subject of the main clause.

- I saw a strange man **with** a parrot sitting on his shoulder.
  肩にオウムを止まらせている変わった男の人を見ました。
- My parents must feel lonely **with** all their children living away from home.
  私の両親は子どもたちがみんな家を出て暮らしているので、寂しいにちがいありません。

Common Mistake 123

✕1 I went to Tokyo by my friend's car.

✕2 We went there by two cars.

by car、by bus、by trainなどとは言えますが、carやbus, trainなどの前に形容詞、名詞、代名詞がつけば、byではなくinを使います。
We can say 'by car', 'by bus', 'by train', etc., but if we put an adjective, noun or pronoun before 'car', 'bus', 'train', etc., then we must say 'in' instead of 'by'.

1 **I went to Tokyo in my friend's car.**
友人の車で東京へ行きました。

2 **We went there in two cars.**
私たちは2台の車でそこへ行きました。

2輪車（オートバイ、自転車など）の場合はonを使います。
We use 'on' when talking about vehicles with two wheels.

- I went home **on** my friend's bicycle.
  友人の自転車で家へ帰りました。

Common Mistake 124

✕1 I killed the cockroach by my slipper.

✕2 I bought it by my own money.

物や道具を使ってという意味で「〜で」と言うときは、with を使います。
We use 'with' when we talk about an object or tool which we use to do something.

1. **I killed the cockroach with my slipper.**
   私はスリッパでゴキブリを殺しました。
2. **I bought it with my own money.**
   私はそれを自分のお金で買いました。

by は動名詞（動詞＋-ing の形）の前で使います。
We use 'by' before the '-ing' form of the verb.

- We opened the can by making a hole in it with some scissors.
  ハサミで穴を開けることで〈そういう方法で〉缶を開けました。

受け身の文では、その動作を行った人や物の前に by を使います。
In passive sentences, 'by' is used before the thing or person which did the action.

- He was hit by a rock.
  彼は石にあたりました。
- I was bitten by a snake.
  私はヘビにかまれました。

Common Mistake 125

✕1 I went to there last year.

✕2 When did you come to here?

✕3 I love Kobe and I want to live in there all my life.

there, here, somewhere, anywhere, nowhereの前には、to, at, inは使いません。

'To', 'at' and 'in' are not used before 'there', 'here', 'somewhere', 'anywhere' or 'nowhere'.

① **I went ∧ there last year.**
私は去年そこへ行きました。

② **When did you come ∧ here?**
ここへはいついらしたのですか。

③ **I love Kobe and I want to live ∧ there all my life.**
私は神戸が好きで、一生そこに住みたいと思います。

例外として、there, hereが箱、戸棚、部屋など立体的なものの中を指す場合は、in there, in hereと言います。

There is one exception to the above rule. We can say 'in there' and 'in here' when 'there' and 'here' refer to an enclosed three-dimensional space such as a box, cupboard, room, etc.

- There's a red box on top of the piano, and the key is in there.
  ピアノの上に赤い箱があり、かぎはその中にあります。

Common Mistake 126

~~1~~ I went back ∧ my hometown.

~~2~~ I want to go back ∧ Canada one day.

backは前置詞ではなく副詞なので、名詞の前ではtoが必要です。
'Back' is an adverb, not a preposition, so we must say 'back to' before a noun.

① **I went back to my hometown.**
私は故郷へ帰りました。

② **I want to go back to Canada one day.**
私はいつかカナダへ帰りたい。

しかし、home, here, thereの前ではtoを使わず、back home, back here, back thereと言います。
However, 'to' is not used before 'home', 'here' and 'there', so we can say 'back home', 'back here' and 'back there'.

- He went **back home**.
  彼は家へ帰りました。
- Please come **back here** tomorrow.
  どうぞ明日ここへ戻って来てください。
- I have to go **back there** tomorrow.
  私は明日そこへ帰らなければなりません。

注意したいのはhomeの前にそれを説明する言葉があるときで、その場合はtoを使います。
Note that we must use 'to' if 'home' is preceded by a word which describes it.

- He went back **to** his parents' home.
  彼は両親の家へ帰りました。

'go'と'come'の違いについてはCommon Mistake 27を参照。
For the difference between 'go' and 'come', see *Common Mistake 27*.

Common Mistake **127**

✕ I want to go to abroad next year.

abroad「外国へ［に］」は副詞なので、その前にtoを置くことはできません。
'Abroad' is an adverb, so we cannot put 'to' in front of it.

○ **I want to go ∧ abroad next year.**
私は来年外国へ行きたい。

Common Mistake 128

~~1~~ Every summer I go swimming to the sea.

~~2~~ I went shopping to Umeda.

~~3~~ I went skiing to Nagano Prefecture.

go swimming, go shopping, go skiingなどの表現のあとではtoは使わず、ふつうinを使います。
We do not use 'to' after expressions such as 'go swimming', 'go shopping', 'go skiing', etc. Instead, we usually say 'in'.

1. **Every summer I go swimming in the sea.**
   毎年夏は海へ泳ぎに行きます。
2. **I went shopping in Umeda.**
   私は梅田へ買い物に行きました。
3. **I went skiing in Nagano Prefecture.**
   私は長野県へスキーに行きました。

beach, road, lakeなどの表面を表す名詞の前ではonを使います。
'On' is used before a noun referring to a surface.

- We went sailing on Lake Biwa.
  私たちは、琵琶湖でヨットに乗りました。

Common Mistake 129

✗1 the house's roof

✗2 the street's end

✗3 the parade's photographs

ふつう、生物以外のものについて「〜の」という意味を表すときは、ー's の形でなくofを使います。

Generally speaking, we do not use the –'s genitive with things which are not living, so we should say:

1. **the roof** of the house
   家の屋根
2. **the end** of the street
   通りの突き当たり
3. **the photographs** of the parade
   パレードの写真

しかし例外として次の生物以外のものには、ー'sの形が使えます。

However there are some exceptions to this rule. We can use the –'s genitive with the following non-living things:

1. 市、国、地域などの場合
   cities, countries, regions, etc.

- Tokyo's population (*or* 'the population of Tokyo')
  東京の人口
- America's natural resources (*or* 'the natural resources of America')
  アメリカの天然資源

2. 乗り物の場合
vehicles

- **the car's** wheels (*or* 'the wheels **of the car**')
  車の車輪
- **the plane's** wings (*or* 'the wings **of the plane**')
  飛行機の翼

3. 人の組織――政府、会社、大学、クラブなどの場合
human organizations, i.e. governments, companies, universities, clubs, etc.

- **the government's** decision (*or* 'the decision **of the government**')
  政府の決定
- **the company's** president (*or* 'the president **of the company**')
  会社の社長

4. 時間を表現する語の場合
time expressions

- **today's** newspaper
  今日の新聞
- **two weeks'** holiday
  2週間の休暇

Common Mistake 130

✕1 the house of my parents

✕2 the car of Mr. Nakano

人の所有物について「〜の」と言うときは、ふつうofではなく−'sの形を使います。

We usually use the –'s genitive, not 'of', when we talk about a person's possessions.

1 **my parents' house**
私の両親の家

2 **Mr. Nakano's car**
中野さんの車

しかし、その人物についての説明の句や節があとにあるときは、ofを使います。

However, we use 'of' with a noun referring to a person when it is followed by a phrase or clause describing it.

- What's the name of that woman over there?
あそこにいる女性の名前は何ですか。

- He is the great-grandson of an Irish couple who came to the United States in 1905.
彼は1905年にアメリカに来たアイルランド人夫婦のひ孫です。

Common Mistake 131

✕ I am very impatient, as my father.

2人の人や2つのものが似ていることを表そうとするとき、名詞、代名詞（そのあとに動詞がなければ）の前では前置詞likeを使います。

When we want to say that two people or things are similar, we use 'like' before a noun or pronoun which is not followed by a verb. 'Like' is a preposition.

 **I am very impatient, like my father.**

父と同じように、私もとても短気です。

動詞がある節の前では、asを使います。くだけた英語では、likeも節の前でよく使われます。

We use 'as' before a clause containing a verb. In informal English 'like' is often used before a clause.

- I wanted to travel abroad, as my brother had done.
  兄がかつてしたように、私も海外旅行をしたかったです。
- Nobody could dance like he could.
  彼と同じように踊れる人はだれもいませんでした。

Common Mistake **132**

✕1 I don't have any brothers and sisters.

✕2 We had nothing to eat and drink.

not, never, nothing, nobody などの打ち消しの語のあとでは、andではなくorを使います。

After a negative word such as 'not', 'never', 'nothing', 'nobody', etc., we say 'or', not 'and'.

① **I don't have any brothers or sisters.**

私には兄弟も姉妹もいません。

② **We had nothing to eat or drink.**

食べる物も飲む物もありませんでした。

Common Mistake **133**

✗1 She went out in spite of it was raining heavily.

✗2 He came to the lesson despite he was very ill.

動詞を含む節の前ではalthoughやeven thoughを使います。in spite ofとdespiteは、あとに動詞が続いていない名詞や代名詞の前で使います。

'Although' and 'even though' are used before clauses containing a verb. 'In spite of' and 'despite' are used before nouns and pronouns which are not followed by a verb.

1. **She went out even though it was raining heavily.**
   She went out in spite of the heavy rain.
   雨が激しく降っていたのに、彼女は出かけました。
2. **He came to the lesson although he was very ill.**
   病気だったにもかかわらず、彼は授業に来ました。

Exercise 6

次の文中の間違いを見つけて正しい英語に直してください。それぞれの文末のかっこ内の数は、間違いの数を示しています。答えは巻末にあります。

1. I read a lot of books during I was ill. (1)

2. I couldn't sleep in spite of I was very tired. (1)

3. I love listening to the music, as my mother. (2)

4. I'm going to New York in next month. (1)

5. My grandparents live at Shikoku. (1)

6. We went to sea by my car. (2)

7. He hit the dog by stick. (2)

8. I have to finish this report until 5 p.m. in Friday afternoon. (2)

9. I put a sign on my room's door saying 'Do not disturb'. (1)

10. I go back my hometown after four days. (3)

11. He cannot read and write. (1)

12. My father often goes to abroad on business. (1)

13. I want to go to there one day. (1)

14. I read much with sitting in the train. (2)

15. I went shopping to Shibuya. (1)

16. I usually see my boyfriend once or twice in a week. (1)

Chapter 7

その他の間違い

Miscellaneous Problems

Common Mistake 134

✗1 I look like ∧ mother.

✗2 ∧ Father is very kind.

「私の母、父」と言いたいとき、アメリカ英語では、家族内で話したり手紙を書いたりする場合はmotherやfatherにmyをつけないで言うこともできます。しかし家族以外の人に話したり手紙を書いたりする場合はmyをつけたほうがよいでしょう。

In American English it is possible to say 'mother' and 'father' without 'my' when talking or writing about one's own mother or father to a close family member. However, if one is talking or writing to someone other than a close family member, it is better to say 'my mother' and 'my father'.

1 **I look like my mother.**

私は母親似です。

2 **My father is very kind.**

父はとても優しい。

イギリス英語では、自分の両親について話すときはいつでもmy father, my motherというようにmyがつきます。

In British English, one always says 'my father' and 'my mother' when talking about one's own father and mother.

Common Mistake 135

~~1~~ I am looking for my job.

~~2~~ I want to buy my car.

ものが自分の所有物になる前（買う前、手に入れる前）は、それにmyをつけることはできません。

We cannot say 'my job' before we have got it. We cannot say 'my car' before we have bought it.

1 **I am looking for a job.**

私は仕事を探しています。

2 **I want to buy a car.**

私は車を買いたい。【買えばmy carになる】

Common Mistake 136

✗1 Japanese rice is more expensive than American one.

✗2 I prefer French food to Japanese one.

代名詞oneが取って代われるのは、数えられる名詞だけです。riceやfoodは数えられない名詞なので、oneを代わりに置くことはできません。
The pronoun 'one' can only replace a countable noun. In the sentences above, 'rice' and 'food' are uncountable, so they cannot be replaced by 'one'.

1 Japanese rice is more expensive than American rice.
日本の米はアメリカの米より高い。

2 I prefer French food to Japanese food.
私は日本料理よりフランス料理のほうが好きです。

- This sweater's too small. Do you have a bigger one?
  このセーターは小さすぎます。もっと大きいものはありますか。
  【sweaterは数えられる名詞】

Common Mistake 137

✗1 I want to go to Hokkaido. There is beautiful, and cool in summer.

✗2 Last year I went to London. I liked there very much.

すでに話に出てきた場所を指して「そこは」「そこが」と言いたいときは、thereではなくitを使います。主語や目的語としてthereを使うことはできません。

We cannot use 'there' as the subject or object of a verb when we are referring to a place which we have already mentioned. Instead we say 'it'.

① **I want to go to Hokkaido. It is beautiful, and cool in summer.**
私は北海道へ行きたい。そこは美しいし夏は涼しい。

② **Last year I went to London. I liked it very much.**
昨年私はロンドンへ行きました。私はそこがとても気に入りました。

there is 〜 は話の中に何かを初めて持ち出すときに使います。
We use 'there is' when we are introducing something for the first time.

- **There is** a small lake in the middle of the wood.
森の真ん中には小さな湖があります。

7 その他の間違い

Common Mistake 138

✗1 There is Mount Fuji in Shizuoka Prefecture.

✗2 There is the sea near my house.

✗3 There is my favorite girl in this class.

次の文型は使えません。
1. There is＋固有名詞＋場所
2. There is＋theのついた名詞＋場所
3. There is＋所有形容詞（my、your、hisなど）のついた名詞＋場所

それぞれ次のように言います。

We cannot say any of the following structures:
1. 'There is' + proper noun + expression of place
2. 'There is' + 'the' + noun + expression of place
3. 'There is' + possessive adjective ('my', 'your', 'his', etc.) + noun + expression of place

Instead, we say:

① **Mount Fuji is in Shizuoka Prefecture.**
富士山は静岡県にあります。

② **The sea is near my house.**
私の家の近くに海があります。

My house is near the sea.
私の家は海の近くです。

③ **My favorite girl is in this class.**
僕の一番好きな女の子はこのクラスにいます。

there isは、特定の人や物を表していない名詞とともに使います。例えば次の例文のa spiderは、特定のクモを表しているわけではないので、there isを使います。

We use 'there is' with an indefinite noun, that is, a noun that does not represent a particular thing or person. For example, in the sentence below, 'a spider' does not represent any particular spider.

- There's a spider in the bath.
  お風呂の中にクモがいます。

何かを指して言うときにも、there is＋固有名詞や、theのついた名詞、所有形容詞の形が使えます。

We can use 'there is' + a proper noun or 'the' or a possessive adjective when we are pointing at something.

- Look! There's Mount Fuji!
  ほら！　富士山だ！

- Look! There's the sea!
  見てごらん！　海だよ！

文や節が場所を表す言葉で始まるときは、次の文型が使えます。この文型は主に英語の書き言葉に見られます。

1. 場所＋there is＋固有名詞
2. 場所＋there is＋theのついた名詞

If a sentence or clause begins with an expression of place, it is possible to say (1) 'there is' + a proper noun, or (2) 'there is' + 'the' + a noun. This structure is mainly found in writing.

- To the west there are the Yoro Mountains, and to the east there are three rivers.
  西には養老の山々、東には３本の川があります。

Common Mistake 139

✗1 Every summer I go to the mountains, where is cool.

✗2 There are many places in Japan where I like.

関係副詞whereは「そこで」「そこに」「そこへ」という意味です。節の主語や目的語になることはできません。

The relative adverb ‘where’ cannot be the subject or object of a verb. It means ‘in which’ or ‘at which’ or ‘to which’.

1 **Every summer I go to the mountains, where it is cool.**

毎夏、私は山へ行きます。そこはとても涼しいです。

2 **There are many places in Japan which I like.**

日本には私の好きなところがたくさんあります。

- I went to Okinawa, **where** my grandparents live.

  私は沖縄へ行きました。そこには祖父母が住んでいます。

Common Mistake 140

✗1 We were seven persons in the car.

✗2 My family is five.

✗3 The club's members are 55.

人や物の数は、《There are＋数》で表します。
We say 'there are + a number' to express the number of people or things.

① **There were seven of us in the car.**
その車には私たち7人が乗っていました。

There were seven people in the car.
その車には7人乗っていました。

② **There are five people in my family.**
There are five of us in my family.
わが家は5人家族です。

③ **There are 55 members in the club.**
クラブの人数は55人です。

また、グループになっている人や物の数を表すときは、動詞のconsistを使うこともできます。
Alternatively, if we are talking about a group of people or things, we can use the verb 'consist'.

- My family **consists of five people.**
  私の家族は5人です。
- The club **consists of 55 members.**
  クラブ員は55人います。

Common Mistake 141

~~1~~ I don't know what should I do.

~~2~~ Do you know where does he live?

~~3~~ I wonder why was she angry.

従属節の語順は疑問形ではなく、常に肯定形です（従属節とは、文の一部分の節のことで、例えば、下の例文ではwhat I should doです）。

The word order of questions is not used in subordinate clauses. In a subordinate clause the subject always comes before the verb, and the auxiliary verb 'do' is not used. (A subordinate clause is a clause which is part of a sentence. For example, in the sentence below, 'what I should do' is a subordinate clause.)

1. **I don't know what I should do.**
   何をすべきなのか私にはわかりません。
2. **Do you know where he lives?**
   彼がどこに住んでいるのか知っていますか。
3. **I wonder why she was angry.**
   彼女はなぜ腹を立てたのだろうか。

Common Mistake 146

~~1~~ *A:* May I smoke?

B: Please.

~~2~~ *A:* Do you mind if I open the window?

B: Please.

please は日本語の「どうぞ」と同じではありません。May I ～ ?、Can I ～ ?という表現で許可を求められたときの返事は、Please. ではなく、Yes, sure. や Yes, of course. です。よりていねいにしたければ Yes, certainly. と言います。

'Please' is not the same as *dozo*. If someone asks us for permission to do something using the expression 'May I ～ ?' or 'Can I ～ ?', we reply 'Yes, sure' or 'Yes, of course' or if we wish to be more polite, 'Yes, certainly'.

① ***A:* May I smoke?**

たばこを吸ってもいいですか。

***B:* Yes, sure.**

どうぞ。

Do/Would you mind if ～ ?という表現で許可を求められ、「どうぞ」と答えたいときは No, go ahead. または Sure. と言います。

If someone asks us for permission using the expression 'Do you mind if ～ ?' or 'Would you mind if ～ ?', and if we wish to give permission, we say 'No, go ahead' or 'Sure'.

＊mind は「気にする、迷惑に思う」という意味です。Do/Would you mind if ～ ?は「私が～するのは迷惑ではありませんか」(＝「～してもいいですか」) という意味になるので、返事の「迷惑ではありません」(＝「どうぞ」) には No が必要です。

② ***A:* Do you mind if I open the window?**

窓を開けてもいいですか。

***B:* No, go ahead.**

どうぞ。

人に物を渡すときの「はい、どうぞ」はPlease.ではなくHere you are.です。「どうぞお先に」もPlease.ではなくAfter you.です。

When we give things to people, we say 'Here you are.' not 'Please'. When we ask someone to go through a door before us, or to do something before us, we say 'After you' not 'Please'.

「どうぞお入りください」と客を家や部屋の中へ通すときは、Come in.と言います。「どうぞお座りください」は、Have a seat.とかTake a seat.です。それらの前にpleaseをつけると、よりていねいになりますが、一言だけPlease.とは言いません。pleaseは、頼みや指図をていねいにするために使います。

When inviting someone to come into a house or room, we say 'Come in' or 'Please come in'. We do not say simply 'Please'. When asking someone to sit down, we say 'Have a seat' or 'Take a seat'. If we want to be more polite, we say 'Please have a seat' or 'Please take a seat', but we do not say simply 'Please'. We use 'please' with requests and orders to make them more polite, for example:

- **Please** wait a moment.
  少々お待ちください。
- Could you buy some stamps, **please**?
  切手を買ってきていただけませんか。

人にすすめられたものをもらいたいときは、Yes, please. か、Please. とだけ言います。

We say 'Yes, please' (or sometimes simply 'Please') if we want something which has been offered to us.

- *A:* Would you like some more tea?
  もっとお茶をいかがですか。

  B: **Yes, please.**
  はい、いただきます。

Common Mistake 147

~~1~~ *A:* Did you not have a lesson this morning?

B: Yes, I played tennis instead.

~~2~~ *A:* You don't smoke, do you?

B: Yes, I stopped last month.

否定疑問文に答えるとき、「はい、その通りです」と答えたければNo.と言います。否定疑問文とは、not, never, no, nothing, nobody, no-one, nowhere, none, neitherなどの語を含む疑問文のことです。反対に「いいえ、違います」と答えたければYes.と言います。

When we are answering a negative question, the word 'no' means 'That's right'. A negative question is a question which contains one of the following words: not, never, no, nothing, nobody, no-one, nowhere, none, neither, etc. 'Yes' means 'That's wrong.' when we are answering a negative question.

1 ***A:* Did you not have a lesson this morning?**

今朝、授業はなかったのですか。

***B:* No, I played tennis instead.**

ええ、その代わりにテニスをしました。

2 ***A:* You don't smoke, do you?**

たばこは吸わないのですね。

***B:* No, I stopped last month.**

はい、先月やめました。

- *A:* You don't smoke, do you?

  たばこは吸わないのですね。

B: Yes, I do, actually.
いいえ、実は吸います。

Common Mistake **148**

✕1 *A:* How long have you been in Japan?

B: Six months.

A: How about Japanese food?

✕2 Dear Mr. Webb,

How about your holiday?

How about ～ ?は「～についてどう思いますか」という意味ではありません（ただし後述の特定の場合を除きます）。これらは次のように表現します。
'How about' does not mean 'What is your opinion of～ ?' except in certain situations. (See below.) One should say:

① ***A:* How long have you been in Japan?**
日本にいらしてどのくらいになりますか。

***B:* Six months.**
6カ月です。

***A:* Do you like Japanese food?**
日本の食事は好きですか［いかがですか］。

② **Dear Mr. Webb,**

How was your holiday?
ウェブ様　休暇はいかがでしたか。【手紙の書き出し】

How about ～？は、気軽な提案として使います。

'How about' is used in informal suggestions.

- **How about** a drink?

  何か飲み物はいかがですか。

- **How about** going to have a drink?

  飲みに行きませんか。

また、How aboutは、たった今言った質問や提案の一部分の代わりとしても使い、質問文を短くしています。

'How about' is also used in short questions as a substitute for part of a longer question or suggestion which has just been said. For example:

- *A:* Do you like Japanese food?

  日本食はお好きですか。

  B: Yes, I do.

  はい、好きです。

  A: **How about** raw fish? (= Do you like raw fish?)

  おさしみはいかがですか。

- *A:* Shall we go and see a movie tomorrow evening?

  明日の夜、映画を見に行きましょうか。

  B: I'm sorry, I'm busy tomorrow. **How about** Saturday?
  (= Shall we go and see a movie on Saturday?)

  ごめんなさい、明日は忙しいの。土曜日はどうかしら。

Common Mistake 149

✕ Osaka and Fukui, my hometown, are very different. Osaka is big and crowded and there are few green spaces, but Fukui is smaller and surrounded by mountains.
By the way, the people in Osaka are different from the people in Fukui.

前の話題に関係のあることを付け加えたいときは、by the wayではなくalsoやin additionを使います。
If we want to add a point which is related to what came before, we say ‘also’ or ‘in addition’, not ‘by the way’.

◯ **Osaka and Fukui, my hometown, are very different. Osaka is big and crowded and there are few green spaces, but Fukui is smaller and surrounded by mountains.**
Also, the people in Osaka are different from the people in Fukui.

大阪と私の出身地の福井は、とても違います。大阪は大きく、人が混み合っていて、緑が少ないところです。福井はもっと小さくて、山に囲まれています。
また、大阪の人は福井の人とは違います。

by the wayは、今まで話していたこととは関係のない新しい話題を持ち出すときに使います。
We use ‘by the way’ to introduce a new subject which has no connection with what came before. For example:

● *A:* I think it's going to rain this afternoon.
今日の午後は雨になりそうですね。

B: Yes. By the way, have you seen David recently?
そうですね。ところで最近デイビッドに会いましたか。

また、by the wayは会話や形式的ではない手紙で使います。作文やビジネスレターなどの正式な文書では使いません。
We use 'by the way' in conversation and in informal letters. It should not be used in formal writing such as compositions and business letters.

Common Mistake 150

✕1 I met a friend of mine after a long time.

✕2 I went back to my hometown after a long time.

「久しぶり」と英語で言いたいときは、次のような言い方をします。
There is no word in English which means exactly the same as *hisashiburi*. We should say:

1 **I met a friend of mine who I hadn't seen for a long time.**
久しぶりに友人に会いました。

2 **I went back to my hometown for the first time in ages.**
I went back to my hometown after a long absence.
久しぶりに故郷へ帰りました。

久しぶりに会った相手には、次のように言います。
When we meet someone who we have not seen for a long time, we say to him or her:

● **I haven't seen you for ages.**
お久しぶりですね。

くだけた状況のときには、次のようにも言えます。
Alternatively, in an informal situation we say:

● **Long time no see.**
久しぶり！

Common Mistake 151

~~1~~ What are you going to do at X'mas?

~~2~~ X'mas is very popular in Japan.

Xmas（クリスマス）はふつう、アポストロフィ（'）はつけず、友達や親戚あての手紙や、広告などのような、とてもくだけた場合の書き言葉としてしか使われません。もう少し正式な場合は、XmasではなくChristmasと書きます。

'Xmas' is usually written without an apostrophe, and it is only used in very informal writing such as letters to friends and relatives, advertisements, etc. In more formal writing one should write 'Christmas', not 'Xmas'.

1. **What are you going to do at Xmas?**
   クリスマスは何をするのですか。
2. **Christmas is very popular in Japan.**
   クリスマスは日本ではとてもさかんです。

Exercise 7

次の文中の間違いを見つけて正しい英語に直してください。それぞれの文末のかっこ内の数は、間違いの数を示しています。答えは巻末にあります。

1. I want to live in Hawaii, where is always warm. (1)

2. I want to visit San Francisco. There is very beautiful city. (2)

3. We are five persons in my family. (2)

4. I'm sorry to be late. (1)

5. She looked very sad and lonely, so I thought she was pity. (1)

6. Do you know where is the station? (1)

7. I wonder why didn't he come to the party. (1)

8. I met my high school friends after a long time. (1)

9. I want to buy my motorbike in this summer. (2)

10. There is Himeji Castle near my house. (1)

11. Japanese pop music is very different from American one. (1)

____

12. The people at the meeting were 135. (1)

____

13. I love X'mas. (1)

____

14. I think I want to get a good job with a high salary. (1)

____

Answers

答え

Exercise 1 (p. 25)

1. Japanese **trains are** often crowded.
2. I love **peaches**.
3. Japanese people **are** always busy.
4. She always wears ∧ jeans.
5. I was very busy doing **homework** in the vacation.
6. **Fruit** is very expensive.
7. The police **have** not caught the murderer yet.
8. It is one of the most beautiful **places** I have ever visited.
9. I like all kinds of food—**meat**, **fish**, vegetables, etc.
10. I eat fried **chicken** almost every day.
11. The number of **fish** in the world's oceans is decreasing.
12. I always try not to waste **paper**.
13. **Houses**, **furniture**, newspapers, magazines and books are all made from **wood**.

Exercise 2 (p. 35)

1. When I was **a** high school student, I belonged to **the / a** baseball club.
2. Last summer I had **a** part-time job as **a** waitress in **a** restaurant.
3. We stayed in **a** small hotel by **the** sea.
4. Please put it on **the** top shelf of **the** cupboard.
5. We had ∧ dinner in **an / the** Italian restaurant.
6. I'll wait for you at **the** entrance of **the** cinema.
7. My father gave me **some** good / **a** good **piece of** advice.
8. I am **the** same height as my mother.
9. My parents were born before ∧ World War II.

Exercise 3 (p. 97)

1. I'm going to meet / meeting my friend at 7 o'clock this evening and we're going to see a movie.
2. I lived in London from 1979 to 1981.
3. I went to Nagano last week.
4. Japan has changed very much since the war.
5. Her purse was stolen. *or* She had her purse stolen.
6. I joined the baseball club in April. *or* I've belonged to the baseball club since April.
7. I began / came to like studying English.
8. She married ∧ a foreigner.
9. I enjoyed myself / it very much.
10. I hope you are successful.
11. Every autumn the leaves turn red.
12. Japanese businessmen have no time to relax and enjoy themselves / free time.
13. My grandfather died in the war.
14. Please tell me your address.
15. I have many happy memories when I look at / see the photographs of last summer.
16. She gave me some chocolate on Valentine's Day.
17. It costs a lot of money to rent / hire a wedding kimono.
18. When I was a child, I liked drawing / to draw pictures.
19. I'm trying to learn German.
20. After climbing for four hours, we reached / managed to reach / were able to reach the top of the mountain.
21. I started doing / learning judo when I was a junior high school student.
22. I learned many interesting things by talking with him.

23. She left / quit her job in order to have a baby.
24. I wore a black kimono at the funeral.
25. I don't feel well because I've caught / have a cold.
26. He ran away from home when he was a teenager.
27. I am often told that I look very young.
28. My car skidded on some ice.
29. I have been going out with my girlfriend for two years.
30. I've picked out the three most important points in this book.
31. I wanted to go on a trip with my boyfriend, but my parents didn't allow / let me.
32. Our team beat the other team.
33. Speaking Chinese is very difficult. *or* It is very difficult to speak Chinese.
34. The job doesn't suit me.
35. John Lennon was brought up by his aunt.
36. My mother got angry with me.
37. If I were / was a man, I could get a higher salary.
38. I want to get a driver's license.
39. She had a baby recently.
40. *Yakitori* means 'grilled chicken'.
41. I had many good experiences in Australia. *or* I have many good memories of Australia.
42. The food we eat contains a lot of sugar and chemicals.
43. I went / went on a trip to Hawaii.
44. He has / He's got AIDS.
45. I stopped smoking because I don't want to get cancer.
46. I long / I'd love to go to Europe.
47. I stayed with a family in New Zealand.
48. Studying Chinese is difficult, but I'm going to do the best I can /

I'm really going to try hard.

49. He said 'Good luck' to me before the exam.
50. I am interested in European culture.
51. I haven't decided what I am going to do.

Exercise 4 (p. 132)

1. I was very excited when I heard the news.
2. I always feel embarrassed when I have to give a speech.
3. America is very big / large.
4. There are many parks in London.
5. There are a lot of / lots of / many foreign students at this university.
6. My wages are very low.
7. I think Mr. Takada is very handsome / good-looking.
8. I want to save a lot of / lots of money and buy a car.
9. I was in great pain.
10. In Japan, most ∧ people are tired most of the time.
11. Most young Japanese girls are shy.
12. The weather was absolutely / really terrible, but we enjoyed ourselves / it very much.
13. The trip was a lot of / good / great / really fun.
14. We talked until 3 a.m. and then, finally, we went home.
15. I have ∧ been to New Zealand.
16. I enjoyed myself / it very much.
17. Nowadays / These days many Japanese people read comics.
18. Swimming in the sea on a hot, sunny day is very enjoyable / very pleasant / (a lot of) fun.
19. I find it very hard to learn German grammar. *or*

I have difficulty learning German grammar. *or*
Learning German grammar is very hard (for me). *or*
I find learning German grammar very hard.

20. I thought I was going to die, so I was really frightened / scared / terrified.
21. I like horror movies because they are frightening / scary / terrifying.
22. He is half-Japanese. *or* One of his parents is Japanese.
23. All Japanese schoolchildren have to learn English. *or*
Every Japanese schoolchild has to learn English.
24. There are too many students in this college, so I feel it is cramped.
25. There are very few / not many English people in Japan.
26. I couldn't understand the teacher, so I was bored.
27. At high school I was really into / crazy about / really keen on music.
28. During ∧ World War II, there was very little / not much food in Japan.

Exercise 5 (p. 161)

1. My hometown is in Hokkaido. *or* My home is in Hokkaido. *or* I come from Hokkaido.
2. My hometown is in the country / countryside. *or* I come from (a small town in) the country / countryside.
3. Many Japanese people go back to their hometown at the New Year.
4. I hate being woken by the telephone at night / in the middle of the night.
5. I had a pleasant trip / journey.
6. Before the war the Japanese / Japanese people were poorer than now.

7. When I was in America I **had a hard time / difficulty eating** American food.
8. There were a lot of **people** in the park.
9. My **hobbies are** music, swimming and **skiing**.
10. Harajuku is **a** very fashionable **district / area** in Tokyo.
11. My mother's **cooking is** delicious.
12. He **works in an office**.
13. The **manager** of the restaurant is very kind.
14. **I love** shopping.
15. The teacher uses **handouts** instead of a textbook.
16. Japanese people throw away a lot of **trash / garbage / rubbish** every day.
17. Please put your **trash / garbage / rubbish** in the **trash can / garbage can / rubbish bin**.
18. Most **soft drinks contain** a lot of sugar and artificial chemicals.
19. Many Japanese people live in **apartments / flats**.
20. He wears **earrings / an earring**.
21. I want to be a **safe** driver.
22. **Britain / The UK / The United Kingdom** has much higher taxes than Japan.
23. I like sending **emails / texts** to my friends. *or*
    I like **emailing / texting** my friends.

Exercise 6 (p. 187)

1. I read a lot of books **while** I was ill.
2. I couldn't sleep **even though / although** I was very tired.
3. I love listening to ∧ music, **like** my mother.
4. I'm going to New York ∧ next month.
5. My grandparents live **in** Shikoku.

6. We went to the sea in my car.
7. He hit the dog with a stick.
8. I have to finish this report by 5 p.m. on Friday afternoon.
9. I put a sign on the door of my room saying ‘Do not disturb’.
10. I’m going back to my hometown in four days / days’ time.
11. He cannot read or write. *or* He can neither read nor write.
12. My father often goes ∧ abroad on business.
13. I want to go ∧ there one day.
14. I read a lot while sitting in the train.
15. I went shopping in Shibuya.
16. I usually see my boyfriend once or twice ∧ a week.

Exercise 7 (p. 213)

1. I want to live in Hawaii, where it is always warm.
2. I want to visit San Francisco. It is a very beautiful city.
3. There are five of us / people in my family. *or*
   My family consists of five people.
4. Sorry I’m late. *or* I’m sorry I’m late.
5. She looked very sad and lonely, so I felt sorry for her.
6. Do you know where the station is?
7. I wonder why he didn’t come to the party.
8. I met my high school friends who I hadn’t seen for a long time / ages.
9. I want to buy a motorbike ∧ this summer.
10. Himeji Castle is near my house.
11. Japanese pop music is very different from American pop music.
12. There were 135 people at the meeting.
13. I love Christmas / Xmas.
14. I ∧ want to get a good job with a high salary.

| 著者紹介 |

ジェイムズ・H・M・ウェブ (James H. M. Webb)

1956年、イギリスに生まれる。オックスフォード大学大学院にてサンスクリット語を専攻し、修士号を取得。1981年より日本、イギリス、イタリアで英語を母語としない人々を対象に英語を教授。現在、関西外国語大学教授。1986年に日本人女性と結婚し、京都に住んでいる。著書に『そのままでは通じない! カタカナ英語のミス』(ジャパンタイムズ出版)、『イギリスってどんな国? —素顔の英国』(実教出版)、『日本人に共通する英語のミス 矯正ドリル』(ジャパンタイムズ出版) がある。

新版 日本人に共通する英語のミス151

2020年10月20日 初版発行

著　者　ジェイムズ・H・M・ウェブ

発行者　伊藤秀樹
発行所　株式会社 ジャパンタイムズ出版
〒102-0082 東京都千代田区一番町2-2 一番町第二TGビル2F
電話 (050)3646-9500 [出版営業部]
ウェブサイト http://jtpublishing.co.jp
印刷所　株式会社光邦

本書の内容に関するお問い合わせは、上記ウェブサイトまたは郵便でお受けいたします。
定価はカバーに表示してあります。

万一、乱丁落丁のある場合は、送料当社負担でお取り替えいたします。
(株) ジャパンタイムズ出版・出版営業部あてにお送りください。

Printed in Japan ISBN978-4-7890-1773-2

本書のご感想をお寄せください。
https://jtpublishing.co.jp/contact/comment/